FEDERAL BENEFITS
FOR
VETERANS, DEPENDENTS, AND SURVIVORS

Updated Edition

THE US DEPARTMENT OF VETERANS AFFAIRS

Skyhorse Publishing

Additional material copyright © 2020 by Skyhorse Publishing, Inc.

No claim is made to material contained in this work that is derived from government documents. Nevertheless, Skyhorse Publishing claims copyright in all additional content, including, but not limited to, compilation copyright and the copyright in and to any additional material, elements, design, images, or layout of whatever kind included herein.

All inquiries should be addressed to Skyhorse Publishing, 307 West 36th Street, 11th Floor, New York, NY 10018.

Skyhorse Publishing books may be purchased in bulk at special discounts for sales promotion, corporate gifts, fund-raising, or educational purposes. Special editions can also be created to specifications. For details, contact the Special Sales Department, Skyhorse Publishing, 307 West 36th Street, 11th Floor, New York, NY 10018 or info@skyhorsepublishing.com.

Skyhorse® and Skyhorse Publishing® are registered trademarks of Skyhorse Publishing, Inc.®, a Delaware corporation.

Visit our website at www.skyhorsepublishing.com.

10 9 8 7 6 5 4 3 2 1

Library of Congress Cataloging-in-Publication Data is available on file.

Print ISBN: 978-1-5107-4425-7
Ebook ISBN: 978-1-5107-4426-4

Cover design by Richard Rossiter

Printed in the United States of America

Phone Numbers

Veterans Crisis Line. . . . . .1-800-273-8255 and Press 1
Bereavement Counseling. 1-202-461-6530
Civilian Health and Medical Program (CHAMPVA). 1-800-733-8387
Caregiver Stipend 1-877-733-7927
Debt Management Center... 1-800-827-0648
Education. 1-888-442-4551
Foreign Medical Program... 1-303-331-7590
Spina Bifida Program 1-888-820-1756
Camp Lejeune Family Member Program 1-866-372-1144
Headstones and Markers.. 1-800-697-6947
Health Care.. 1-877-222-8387
Homeless Veterans. 1-877-424-3838
Home Loans.. 1-888-827-3702
Life Insurance. 1-800-669-8477
National Cemetery Scheduling Office 1-800-535-1117
Pension Management Center. 1-877-294-6380
Presidential Memorial Certificate Program. 1-202-565-4964
Telecommunication Device for the Deaf (TDD).. 1-800-829-4833
VA Benefits. 1-800-827-1000
VA Combat Call Center 1-877-927-8387
Women Veterans. 1-877-222-8387

Web Sites

Mental Health. . . . . www.mentalhealth.va.gov
Burial and Memorial Benefits . . . . www.cem.va.gov
Caregiver Support . . . . www.caregiver.va.gov
CHAMPVA . . . . https://www.va.gov/COMMUNITYCARE/programs/dependents/
champva/index.asp
Community Care. . . . . https://www.va.gov/communitycare/
eBenefits. . . . . www.ebenefits.va.gov
Education Benefits.. . . . . .www.gibill.va.gov
Environmental Exposures. . . . . www.publichealth.va.gov/exposures
Federal Recovery Coordination Program . . . . www.va.gov/icbc/frcp
Health Care Eligibility . . . . .www.va.gov/healthbenefits
Homeless Veterans... . . . . .www.va.gov/homeless
Home Loan Guaranty . . . . www.homeloans.va.gov
Life Insurance. . . . . .www.insurance.va.gov
Memorial Certificate .Program. . . . . www.cem.va.gov/pmc.asp
My HealtheVet. . . . . www.myhealth.va.gov
National Resource Directory. . . . . .www.nrd.gov
Records. . . . . www.archives.gov/st-louis/military-personnel
Returning Servicemembers . . . . .www.oefoif.va.gov
State Departments of Veterans Affairs . . . . www.va.gov/statedva.htm
Women Veterans. . . . . .www.womenshealth.va.gov
VA Vet Centers. . . . . www.vetcenter.va.gov
VA Home Page. . . . . www.va.gov
VA Benefit Payment Rates. www.vba.va.gov/bln/21/rates
VA Forms. . . . . www.va.gov/vaform
Vocational Rehabilitation and Employment. . . . . .www.vetsuccess.gov

Introduction

Veterans of the United States armed forces may be eligible for a broad range of benefits and services provided by the U.S. Department of Veterans Affairs (VA). These benefits are codified in Title 38 of the United States Code. This booklet contains a brief overview of the most commonly sought information concerning Veterans benefits and services. For the most accurate information, Veterans and family members should visit the websites provided within this publication as regulations, payments, and eligibility requirements are subject to change. For additional information, please visit www.va.gov. To find the nearest VA facility, go to https://www.va.gov/landing2_locations.htm.

General Eligibility: Eligibility for most VA benefits is based upon discharge from active military service under other than dishonorable conditions. Active service means full-time service, other than active duty for training, as a member of the Army, Navy, Air Force, Marine Corps, Coast Guard, or as a commissioned officer of the Public Health Service, Environmental Science Services Administration or National Oceanic and Atmospheric Administration, or its predecessor, the Coast and Geodetic Survey.

Eligible Wartime Periods: Certain VA Benefits Require Wartime Service. For information on eligible wartime periods please visit http://www.benefits.va.gov/pension/wartimeperiod.asp. Dishonorable and bad conduct discharges issued by general courts-martial may bar VA benefits. Veterans in prison must contact VA to determine eligibility. VA benefits will not be provided to any Veteran or dependent wanted for an outstanding felony warrant.

Important Documents: In order to expedite benefits delivery, Veterans seeking a VA benefit for the first time must submit a copy of their service discharge form (DD-214, DD-215, or for World War II Veterans, a WD form), which documents service dates and type of discharge, or provides full name, military service number, and branch and dates of service. The Veteran's service discharge form should be kept in a safe location accessible to the Veteran and next of kin or representative.

The following documents will be needed for claims processing related to a Veteran's death: Veteran's marriage certificate for claims of a surviving spouse or children; Veteran's death certificate if the Veteran did not die in a VA health care facility; children's birth certificates or adoption papers to determine children's benefits; or Veteran's birth certificate to determine parents' benefits. For information and updates on VA benefits and services, follow us on Facebook at http://www.facebook.com/VeteransBenefits and/or Twitter http://twitter.com/VAVetBenefits.

eBenefits

eBenefits is a joint VA/Department of Defense (DoD) Web portal that provides resources and self-service capabilities to service members, Veterans, and their families to apply, research, access, and manage their VA and military benefits and personal information through a secure Internet connection.

Through eBenefits Veterans can: apply for benefits, view their disability compensation claim status, access official military personnel documents (e.g., DD Form 214, Certificate of Release or Discharge from Active Duty), transfer entitlement of Post-9/11 GI Bill to eligible dependents (service members only), obtain a VA-guaranteed home loan Certificate of Eligibility, and register for and update direct deposit information for certain benefits. New features are added regularly.

Accessing eBenefits: The portal is located at www.ebenefits.va.gov. Service members or Veterans must register for an eBenefits account at one of two levels: Basic or Premium. A Premium account allows the user to access personal data in VA and DoD systems, as well as apply for benefits online, check the status of claims, update address records, and more. The Basic account allows access to information entered into eBenefits by the service member or Veteran only. Basic accounts cannot access VA or DoD systems.

Reporting Fraud: Help VA's Secretary ensure integrity by reporting suspected fraud, waste or abuse in VA programs or operations.

Report Fraud to:
VA Inspector General Hotline
810 Vermont Avenue, NW Washington, D.C. 20420
E-mail: vaoighotline@va.gov
VAOIG hotline: **1-800-488-8244**
Fax: **(202) 495-5861**

Contents

Health Care   1

Non-Health Care Benefits   14

Burial and Memorial Benefits   63

Health Care

More information on VA health care is available at the following resources: www.va.gov/health, www.va.gov/healthbenefits and VA Health Benefits toll-free 1-877- 222-VETS (8387) Monday through Friday between 8:00 a.m. and 8:00 p.m. EST.

Basic Eligibility: A person who served in the active military, naval, or air service and who was discharged or released under conditions other than dishonorable may qualify for VA health care benefits including qualifying Reserve and National Guard members.

Minimum Duty Requirements: Veterans who enlisted after September 7, 1980, or who entered active duty after October 16, 1981, must have served 24-continuous months or the full period for which they were called to active duty in order to be eligible. This minimum duty requirement may not apply to Veterans discharged for hardship, early out or a disability incurred or aggravated in the line of duty.

Enrollment: Veterans can complete applications for enrollment in VA health care by using one of the options below:
- To apply by phone, call 1-877-222-VETS (8387) Monday through Friday between 8 a.m. and 8 p.m. EST. VA staff members will collect the needed information and process the enrollment application for an enrollment determination.
- When applying online at va.gov, Veterans fill out the application and electronically submit it to VA for processing. VA will search for your supporting documentation through its electronic information systems and will contact you if it is unable to verify your military service.
- The application form can also be downloaded from https://www. va.gov/health-care/apply/application/introduction. Mail the completed form to: Health Eligibility Center ATTN: Enrollment Eligibility Division 2957 Clairmont Road Suite 200 Atlanta, GA 30329-1647
- Apply in person at any VA health care facility or VA regional office. Once enrolled, Veterans can receive health care at VA health care facilities anywhere in the country.

The following four categories of Veterans are not required to enroll, but are urged to do so to permit better planning of health resources:
1. Veterans with a service-connected disability rated at 50 percent or more.

2. Veterans seeking care for a disability the military determined was incurred or aggravated in the line of duty, but which VA has not yet rated, within 12 months of discharge.

3. Veterans seeking care for a service-connected disability only.

4. Veterans seeking registry examinations (ionizing radiation, Agent Orange, Gulf War/Operation Enduring Freedom/ Operation Iraqi Freedom/ Operation New Dawn (OEF/OIF/OND) depleted uranium, airborne hazards and Airborne Hazards and Open Burn Pit Registry).

Priority Groups: During enrollment, each Veteran is assigned to a priority group. VA uses priority groups to balance demand for VA health care enrollment with resources. Changes in available resources may reduce the number of priority groups VA can enroll. If this occurs, VA will publicize the changes and notify affected enrollees. A description of priority groups follows:

Group 1: Veterans with service-connected disabilities rated 50 percent or more; Veterans determined by VA to be unemployable due to service-connected conditions; and Veterans who have been awarded the Medal of Honor.

Group 2: Veterans with service-connected disabilities rated 30 or 40 percent.

Group 3: Veterans who are former Prisoners of War; Veterans awarded the Purple Heart medal; Veterans whose discharge was for a disability incurred or aggravated in the line of duty; Veterans with VA service-connected disabilities rated 10 or 20 percent; and, Veterans awarded special eligibility classification under Title 38, U.S.C., § 1151, "benefits for individuals disabled by treatment or vocational rehabilitation."

Group 4: Veterans who receive increased compensation or pension based on their need for regular aid and attendance or by reason of being permanently housebound; and, Veterans determined by VA to be catastrophically disabled.

Group 5: Nonservice-connected Veterans and non-compensable service-connected Veterans rated by VA as 0-percent disabled and who have an annual income below the VA's geographically-adjusted income limit (based on your resident ZIP code); Veterans receiving VA Pension benefits; and Veterans eligible for Medicaid benefits.

Group 6: Compensable 0 percent service-connected Veterans; Veterans exposed to ionizing radiation during atmospheric testing or during the occupation of Hiroshima and Nagasaki. Project 112/SHAD participants; Veterans who served in the Republic of Vietnam between Jan. 9, 1962 and May 7, 1975; Veterans who served in the Southwest Asia theater of operations from Aug. 2, 1990, through Nov. 11, 1998; Veterans who served in a theater of combat operations after Nov. 11, 1998, as follows: Veterans discharged from active duty on or after Jan. 28, 2003, for five years post discharge; and Veterans who served on active duty at Camp Lejeune for at least 30 days between Aug.1, 1953, and Dec. 31, 1987. Currently enrolled Veterans and new enrollees who served in a theater of combat operations after Nov.11, 1998 and those who were discharged from active duty on or after Jan. 28, 2003, are eligible for the enhanced benefits for five years post discharge.

Note: At the end of this enhanced enrollment priority group placement time period, Veterans will be assigned to the highest priority group their eligibility for which their status at that time qualifies.

Group 7: Veterans with gross household income below the geo-graphically-adjusted VA income limit for their resident location and, who agree to pay copayments.

Group 8: Veterans with gross household incomes above VA national income limit and the geographically-adjusted income limit for their resident location and, who agree to pay copayments. Veterans eligible for enrollment: Noncompensable 0-percent service-connected and are:

Subpriority a: Enrolled as of Jan. 16, 2003, and who have remained enrolled since that date and/or placed in this subpriority due to changed eligibility status.

Subpriority b: Enrolled on or after June 15, 2009, whose income exceeds the current VA national income limits or VA national geographic income limits by 10 percent or less Veterans eligible for enrollment: nonservice-connected and:

Subpriority c: Enrolled as of Jan. 16, 2003, and who remained enrolled since that date and/ or placed in this subpriority due to changed eligibility status.

Subpriority d: Enrolled on or after June 15, 2009 whose income exceeds the current VA national income limits or VA national geo-graphic income limits by 10 percent or less Veterans NOT eligible for enrollment: Veterans not meeting the criteria above:

Subpriority e: Noncompensable 0-percent service-connected (eligible for care of their service-connected condition only).

Subpriority f: Nonservice-connected

VA's income limits change annually and current levels can be located at https://www.va.gov/healthbenefits/apps/explorer/AnnualIncomeLimits/LegacyVAThresholds/Index?FiscalYear=2019.

The VA MISSION Act

On June 6, 2018, the President signed the VA Maintaining Internal Systems and Strengthening Integrated Outside Networks Act (MISSION Act) of 2018. This law strengthens VA's ability to deliver trusted, easy to access, high quality care at VA facilities, virtually through telehealth, and in your community. The law makes several improvements to VA care that begin on June 6, 2019. Under the MISSION Act, VA will:

- Continue to provide you with an excellent health care experience
- Deliver the right care, at the right time, at the right place
- Continue to offer care through telehealth in your home, in a VA facility, or in the community
- Provide more options for health care, including community care and urgent/walk-in care

Eligibility for Community Care

Community care is changing on June 6, 2019. Under the MISSION Act, there are six different eligibility criteria for community care. Meeting any one of these criteria for the specific care you need means you are eligible to elect to receive that care either through direct VA care or a community provider in VA's network:

- The specific care you need is not provided by VA at any facility
- You reside in a U.S. state (AK, HI, or NH) or territory (Guam, American Samoa, Northern Mariana Islands, or U.S. Virgin Islands) that does not have a full-service VA medical facility
- "Grandfathered" eligibility based on residence and the 40-mile eligibility criterion from the Choice program
- The specific care you need is not available within designated access standards
- You and your referring clinician decide it is in your best medical interest to receive the specific care you need in the community
- VA has designated the VA medical service line delivering the specific care you need as not providing care that complies with VA's standards for quality

Urgent Care

VA will offer an urgent/walk-in care benefit for minor injuries and ill-nesses, such as pink eye or ear infections. To be covered by this benefit, you must be enrolled in the VA health care system and have received care from VA within the 24 months prior to seeking this care to be eligible for this benefit.

Eligible Veterans can seek this care from an urgent care facility or walk-in retail health clinic that is part of VA's community provider network, but not all urgent care facilities or walk-in retail health clinics are in VA's network.

As VA implement the MISSION Act, Veterans should continue to talk to their VA health care team or scheduler to get the care they need. For more information, please visit http://missionact.VA.gov.

VA's income limits change annually and current levels can be located at: https://www.va.gov/healthbenefits/apps/explorer/AnnualIncomeLimits/LegacyVAThresholds/Index?FiscalYear=2019.

Community Care

VA offers a variety of health care and services for Veterans through community providers outside of VA. Veterans may be eligible to receive care from a provider in their community when VA cannot provide the care they need. This type of care is known as "community care," and for eligible Veterans, is provided on behalf of and paid for by VA.

These services are provided to Veterans based on certain conditions and eligibility requirements, and in consideration of a Veteran's specific needs and circumstances. Although some changes have taken place with community care recently, Veterans continue to have access to this type of care. The process starts at your VA medical facility.

If you have a question about your specific care needs, contact your VA medical facility. Accessing Community Care begins with scheduling an appointment with your VA provider (doctor). To find the VA facility closest to you access the facility directory at https://www.va.gov/directory/guide/home.asp. For more information on Community Care programs visit, or call 1-866-606-8198.

Meeting the Unique Needs of Women Veterans: VA staff delivers the highest quality health care in a setting that ensures privacy, dignity, and sensitivity. Local VA facilities offer a variety of services, including women's gender-specific health, screening and disease prevention and routine gynecologic services.

Women Veterans are potentially eligible to receive care provided in the community when authorized by VA; however, the decision to use such care is left to the facility providing care. By law, purchased care can only be provided when the treating facility cannot provide the care required or because of geographical inaccessibility.

Contact a local VA facility's Women Veterans Program Manager for more information on available services, call 1-855-VA-WOMEN (1-855-829-6636) or visit www.womenshealth.va.gov/.

Lesbian Gay Bisexual and Transgender (LGBT) Veterans: LGBT Veterans are eligible for the same VA benefits as any other Veteran and will be treated in a welcoming environment. Transgender Veterans will be treated based upon their self-identified gender, including room assignments in residential and inpatient settings. Same-sex couples: VA launched a website to inform Veterans and beneficiaries of the recent changes in the law and procedures involving same-sex marriages. Veterans can learn more about VA's guidance regarding same-sex marriages at www.va.gov/opa/marriage.

Military Sexual Trauma (MST): MST is the term that VA uses to refer to sexual assault or repeated, threatening sexual harassment occurring during a Veteran's military service. VA has expanded eligibility for Veterans in need of mental health care due to sexual assault or sexual harassment to Reservists and National Guard members participating in weekend drill. To receive free treatment related to MST, Veterans do not need a VA service-connected disability. Veterans do not need to have reported the incident when it happened or have other documentation that it occurred. There are no length-of-service requirements to receive care, and some Veterans may be able to receive free MST-related care even if they are not eligible for other VA care. Veterans can learn more about VA's MST-related services online at www.mentalhealth.va.gov/msthome.asp.

OEF/OIF/OND Care Management: Each VA medical center has an Operation Enduring Freedom/Operation Iraqi Freedom/Operation New Dawn (OEF/OIF/OND) Care Management team in place to coordinate patient care activities and ensure that Veterans are receiving patient-centered, integrated care and benefits. Veterans who served in a theater of operations after Nov. 11, 1998, are eligible for an extended period of eligibility for health care for five years after their discharge. In the case of multiple call-ups, the five-year enrollment period begins on the most recent discharge date. This special eligibility includes cost-free health care services and nursing home care for conditions possibly related to military service and enrollment in Priority Group 6 or higher for five years from their date of discharge or release from active duty, unless they are eligible for enrollment in a higher priority group. More information for connecting with OEF/OIF/OND Care Management teams can be found at www.oefoif.va.gov.

Tax Credit: Veterans who are enrolled with VA for their health care meet the standard for minimum health care coverage; therefore, they are not eligible for assistance to lower their cost of health insurance premiums if they chose to purchase additional health insurance outside of their VA health care coverage. Remember, Veterans cannot receive a tax credit for themselves when enrolling within the market-place, if they are currently enrolled with VA for their health care. For the latest information about VA and the health care law, visit www. va.gov/health/aca/FAQ.asp or call **1-877-222-VETS (8387**).

Financial Assessment: Most Veterans not receiving VA disability compensation or pension payments must provide a financial as-sessment upon initial application to determine their eligibility for free medical care, medications and/or travel benefits. This financial information also may be used to determine the Veteran's enrollment priority group.

For more information, visit www.va.gov/healthbenefits/cost/finan-cial_assessment.asp, call toll-free 1-877-222-VETS (8387) Monday through Friday between 8 a.m. and 8 p.m. EST or contact the enroll-ment coordinator at your local VA medical facility. VA's income limits are located at https://www.va.gov/healthbenefits/apps/explorer/ AnnualIncomeLimits/LegacyVAThresholds/Index?FiscalYear=2019.

VA no longer requires enrolled non-service connected and 0-percent non-compensable service connected Veterans to provide their financial information annually. An assessment will continue to be collected from Veterans at the time of application for enrollment. In lieu of the annual financial reporting, VA will confirm the Veteran's financial information using information obtained from the Internal Revenue Service and Social Security Administration.

Medical Services and Medication Copayments: While many Veterans qualify for free health care based on a VA compensable service-connect-ed condition or other special eligibilities, most Veterans are required to complete a financial assessment at the time of enrollment to determine if they qualify for free health care services. Veterans whose income exceeds the VA income limits as well as those who choose not to com-plete the financial assessment at the time of enrollment must agree to pay required copayments for care to become eligible for VA healthcare services. For more information on medical services and copays, visit https://www.va.gov/HEALTHBENEFITS/cost/copays.asp.

Private Health Insurance Billing: Veterans with private health insurance may choose to use these sources of coverage as a supplement to their VA benefits. Veterans are not responsible for paying any remaining balance of VA's insurance claim not paid or covered by their health insurance. By law, VA is obligated to bill health insurance carriers for services provided to treat a Veteran's nonservice-connected conditions. Veterans are asked to disclose all relevant health insurance information to ensure current insurance information is on file, including coverage through a spouse. Any payment received by VA may be used to offset "dollar for dollar" a Veteran's VA copay responsibility. Funds that VA receives from third party health insurance carriers go directly back to VA medical center's operational budget. That money can be used to hire more staff or buy medical equipment to improve Veterans healthcare. Enrolled Veterans can provide or update their insurance information by:

1. Using the online Health Benefits Renewal form (10-10-EZR) at https://www.va.gov/health-care/apply/application/introduction.

2. Calling 1-877-222-VETS (8387) Monday through Friday between 8 a.m. and 8 p.m. EST.

3. Presenting their health insurance card to the clinic clerk or using the self-service kiosks available at their local VA health care facility. VA health care is NOT considered a health insurance plan.

Reimbursement of Travel Costs: Eligible Veterans and non-Veterans may be provided mileage reimbursement or, when medically indicated, special mode transport (e.g., wheelchair van, ambulance), when travel is in relation to VA medical care. Mileage reimbursement is 41.5 cents per mile and is subject to a deductible of $3 for each one-way trip and $6 for a round trip; with a maximum deductible of $18 or the amount after six one-way trips (whichever occurs first) per calendar month. The deductible may be waived when travel is; in relation to a VA compensation or pension examination; by a special mode of transportation; by an eligible non-Veteran; or will cause a severe financial hardship, as defined by current regulatory guidelines.

Eligibility: A Veteran may be eligible for beneficiary travel services if the following criteria are met:
- have a service-connected (SC) rating of 30 percent or more, or
- are traveling for treatment of a SC condition, or
- receive a VA pension, or your income does not exceed the maximum annual VA pension rate, or

- are traveling for a scheduled compensation or pension, or if not otherwise eligible as noted above and;
- have a vision impairment, spinal cord injury or disorder, or a double or multiple amputation who's travel in connection with care provided through a VA special disabilities rehabilitation program (including programs provided by spinal cord injury centers, blind rehabilitation centers and prosthetics rehabilitation centers) if such care is provided on an in-patient basis or during a period in which you are provided with temporary lodging at a facility of the Department to make such care more accessible.

Veterans may qualify for special mode transportation (ambulance, wheelchair van, etc.) if they meet one of the eligibility criteria in the list above, and have a medical condition requiring an ambulance or a specially equipped van as determined by a VA clinician, and the travel is pre-authorized (authorization is not required for emergencies if a delay would be hazardous to life or health). More information on Beneficiary Travel is available at: www.va.gov/healthbenefits/vtp/beneficiary_travel.asp.

Veteran Health Registries: Certain Veterans can participate in a VA health registry and receive free evaluations. VA maintains health registries to provide special health evaluations and health-related information. To participate, contact the environmental health coordinator at the nearest VA health care facility or visit www.publichealth.va.gov/exposures to see a directory which lists environmental health coordinators by state and U.S. territory. Veterans should be aware that a health registry evaluation is not a disability compensation exam. A registry evaluation does not start a claim for compensation and is not required for any VA benefits. No in-person medical evaluation is required to become registered. Veterans not already enrolled in VA health care should contact an environmental health coordinator at a nearby VA facility by visiting the following link: (http://www.publichealth.va.gov/exposures/coordinators.asp) or calling **1-877-222-8387**. To learn more and for a list of current health registries, visit: www.publichealth.va.gov/exposures/benefits/registry-evaluation.asp.

Vet Center Readjustment Counseling Services: VA provides free readjustment counseling services to Veterans who served in a theater of operations (combat zone) through community-based counseling centers, called Vet Centers. Services also are available for their family members regarding military-related issues. Vet Center counselors provide individual, group, marriage, and family readjustment counseling through direct counseling, outreach, and referral, in 300 community-based Vet Centers located in all 50 states, the District of Columbia, Guam, Puerto Rico, and American Samoa. Vet Center staffs are available during normal business hours at toll-free 1-800-905-4675 EST and 1-866-496-8838 PST. For more information, visit www.vetcenter.va.gov.

Home Improvements and Structural Alterations: VA provides up to $6,800 lifetime benefits for service-connected Veterans and up to $2,000 lifetime benefits for nonservice-connected Veterans to make home improvements and/or structural changes necessary for the continuation of treatment or for disability access to the Veterans home and essential lavatory and sanitary facilities. For application information, contact the prosthetic representative at the nearest VA medical center.

Special Eligibility Programs: VA provides comprehensive health care benefits, including outpatient, inpatient, pharmacy, prosthetics, medical equipment, and supplies for certain Korea and Vietnam Veterans' birth children diagnosed with spina bifida (except spina bifida occulta).

Services for Blind and Visually Impaired Veterans: Severely disabled blind Veterans may be eligible for case management services at a VA medical center and for admission to an inpatient or outpatient VA blind or vision rehabilitation program.

Mental Health Care Treatment: Veterans eligible for VA medical care may receive general and specialty mental health treatment as needed. Mental health services are available in primary care clinics (including Home Based Primary Care), general and specialty mental health outpatient clinics, inpatient mental health units, residential rehabilitation and treatment programs, specialty medical clinics, and Community Living Centers. For more information on VA mental health services, visit www.va.gov/healthbenefits/access/mental_health_care.asp and www.mentalhealth.va.gov or contact your local VA health care facility's Enrollment Office.

Veterans Crisis Line: The Veterans Crisis Line is a toll-free, confidential resource that connects Veterans in crisis and their families and friends with qualified, caring VA responders. Veterans and their loved ones can call 1-800-273-8255 and Press 1, chat online at veteranscrisisline.net, or send a text message to 838255 to receive confidential support 24-hours a day, 7-days a week, 365-days a year even if they are not registered with VA or enrolled in VA health care.

The professionals at the Veterans Crisis Line are specially trained and experienced in helping Veterans of all ages and circumstances — from Veterans coping with mental health issues that were never addressed to Veterans struggling with relationships or the transition back to civilian life. European access: Veterans and members of the military community in Europe may dial 0800-1273-8255 or DSN 118. For more information about VA's suicide prevention program, visit: www.Veteranscrisisline.net.

VA Dental Insurance Program: VA would like all Veterans to have access to good oral health care; however, VA is limited to providing dental benefits to those Veterans who meet certain eligibility criteria. To help Veterans who are not eligible for VA dental benefits or need more comprehensive dental care, VA offers enrolled Veterans and beneficiaries of CHAMPVA the opportunity to purchase dental insurance at a reduced cost through its VA Dental Insurance Program (VADIP).

VADIP has been extended for an additional five years, until Dec. 31, 2021 by the VA Dental Insurance Reauthorization Act of 2016. Delta Dental of California and MetLife will be offering private dental insurance plans for enrolled Veterans and beneficiaries of CHAMPVA for VADIP. VADIP provides eligible individuals the opportunity to purchase discounted dental insurance coverage, including diagnostic services, preventive services, endodontic and other restorative services, surgical services and emergency services. Individuals who enroll in one of the dental insurance plans will pay the entire premium in addition to the full cost of any copayments. Enrollment is voluntary and does not affect eligibility for VA outpatient dental services and treatment. The plans are available to eligible individuals in the United States, the District of Columbia, Puerto Rico, Guam, the U.S. Virgin Islands, American Samoa and the Commonwealth of the Northern Mariana Islands. Individuals who were enrolled in VADIP during the pilot period (Jan. 1, 2013 – Jan. 31, 2017) must re-enroll in one of the new plans offered by Delta Dental or MetLife. While the insurance providers will remain the same, plan options, fees and other factors may have changed from those offered during the pilot.

For more information about this program, call toll free 1-877-222-VETS (8387) Monday through Friday between 8 a.m. and 8 p.m. EST or visit www.va.gov/healthbenefits/vadip. Veterans may also review each insurer for specific information regarding their registration, rates and services: Delta Dental at deltadentalins.com/vadip or call 1-855-370-3303; MetLife at metlife.com/VADIP or call 1-888-310-1681.

Long-term Services: VA provides institution based services (nursing home level of care) to Veterans through three national programs: VA owned and operated Community Living Centers (CLC), State Veterans' Homes owned and operated by the states, and the community nursing home program. Each program has admission and eligibility criteria specific to the program. VA is obligated to pay the full cost of nursing home services for enrolled Veterans who need nursing home care for a service-connected disability, or Veterans who have a 70 percent or greater service-connected disability and Veterans with a rating of total disability based on individual un-employability. VA-provided nursing home care for all other Veterans is based on available resources. For more information on Extended Care Services and Geriatrics, visit https://www.va.gov/GERIATRICS/index.asp.

Emergency Medical Care in U.S. Community Facilities: A medical emergency is generally defined as a condition of such a nature that a sensible person would expect that a delay in seeking immediate medical attention would be hazardous to life or health. Eligible Veterans may receive emergency care at a community health care facility, possibly at VA expense, when a VA facility (or other Federal health care facility with which VA has an agreement) cannot furnish efficient care due to the distance from the facility, or when VA is unable to furnish the needed emergency services. Since payment may be limited to the point when the condition is stable enough for the Veteran to travel to a VA facility, a family member or friend must contact the closest VA medical facility within 72 hours of the emergency. The emergency is deemed to have ended when a VA provider has determined that, based on sound medical judgment; the Veteran could be transferred from the community facility to a VA medical center. For more information on urgent care, visit https://www.va.gov/COMMUNITYCARE/programs/Veterans/Emergency_Care.asp.

Foreign Medical Program: VA's Foreign Medical Program (FMP) provides health care payment/reimbursement for U.S. Veterans with VA-rated service-connected conditions who live or travel abroad. Veterans may also register by email at IRIS.va.gov. All other Veterans living or planning to travel outside the U.S. should register with the Foreign Medical Program, P.O. Box 469061, Denver, CO 80246-9061, USA; telephone 303-331-7590. For information, visit: https://www.va.gov/COMMUNITYCARE/programs/Veterans/fmp/index.asp.

Caregiver Programs and Services: The Program of Comprehensive Assistance for Family Caregivers provides certain medical, travel, training and financial benefits to caregivers of certain Veterans and who were seriously injured during their military service on or after Sept.11, 2001. Eligible primary family caregivers can receive a stipend, training, mental health services, travel and lodging reimbursement and access to health insurance if they are not already under a health care plan. For more information, contact your local VA medical facility and speak with a caregiver support coordinator, visit www.caregiver.va.gov or call toll-free at 1-855-260-3274.

Camp Lejeune Family Member Program: The Camp Lejeune Family Member Program (CLFMP) is a medical care cost reimbursement program for family members of Veterans who were stationed at Camp Lejeune between August 1, 1953 through December 31, 1987. VA will reimbursement eligible Camp Lejeune Family Members for health care costs related to one or more of 15 specified illnesses or medical conditions. For more information visit https://www.clfamilymembers.fsc.va.gov or call the toll-free CLFMP customer service line at 1-866-372-1144.

Traveling Veterans: Enrolled Veterans, who receive their health care with VA, will receive the same, coordinated care, whether at their local VA treatment site or an alternate VA site of care. In order to help VA ensure Veterans receive consistent care while they are traveling, Veterans are asked to notify their VA Patient Aligned Care Team (PACT) and specialty care provider(s) four to six weeks before traveling, or as soon as possible. Early planning will allow time for PACT and the Traveling Veteran Coordinator to coordinate care at an alternate VA facility. VA providers at the alternate site will record the care in the Veteran's electronic medical record for follow-up treatment options with their PACT. To coordinate health care with another VA health care facility, Veterans should inform their PACT of the following:
- travel destination(s), and temporary address
- valid telephone number
- arrival and departure dates
- specific care concerns

Their PACT will contact the Traveling Veteran Coordinator, who will assist in coordinating care at the alternate facility. For more information, contact PACT or a Traveling Veteran Coordinator at the local VA facility.

Non-Health Care Benefits

Disability Compensation: Disability compensation is a tax-free monetary benefit paid to Veterans with disabilities that are the result of a disease or injury incurred or aggravated during active military service. The benefits amount is graduated according to the degree of the Veteran's disability on a scale from 10 percent to 100 percent (in increments of 10 percent). Compensation may also be paid for disabilities that are considered related or secondary to disabilities occurring in service and for disabilities presumed to be related to circumstances of military service, even though they may arise after service.

To be eligible for compensation, the Veteran must have been separated or discharged under conditions other than dishonorable. Monthly disability compensation varies with the degree of disability and the number of eligible dependents. Veterans with disability ratings of at least 30 percent are eligible for additional allowances for dependents, including spouses, minor children, children between the ages of 18 and 23 who are attending school, children who are permanently incapable of self-support because of a disability arising before age 18, and dependent parents. The additional amount depends on the disability rating and the number of dependents. For detailed 2019 compensation rate information visit: https://www.benefits.va.gov/COMPENSATION/resources_comp01.asp.

The payment of military retirement pay, disability severance pay and separation incentive payments, known as Special Separation Benefit (SSB) and Reservists' Involuntary Separation Pay (RISP), and Voluntary Separation (VSP), may affect the amount of VA compensation paid to disabled Veterans. For additional details on types of disability claims and how to apply, visit: https://www.benefits.va.gov/compensation/.

Special Monthly Compensation (SMC): SMC is an additional tax-free benefit that can be paid to Veterans as well as their spouses, surviving spouses, and parents. For Veterans, SMC is a higher rate of compensation paid, due to special circumstances such as the need for aid and attendance by another person, or due to a specific disability such as the loss of use of one hand or leg. A Veteran who is determined by VA to be in need of the regular aid and attendance of another person, or a Veteran who is permanently housebound, may be entitled to additional payments. For detailed 2019 special monthly compensation rate information visit: http://www.benefits.va.gov/COMPENSATION/resources_comp02.asp.

Allowance for Aid and Attendance or Housebound Veterans: Veterans and survivors who are eligible for a VA pension and require the aid and attendance of another person, or are housebound, may be eligible for additional monetary payment. These benefits are paid in addition to monthly pension, and they are not paid without eligibility to pension. You may apply for Aid and Attendance or Housebound benefits by writing to the Pension Management Center (PMC) that serves your state. https://www.benefits.va.gov/PENSION/resources-contact.asp. You may also visit your local regional benefit office to file your request. You can locate your local regional benefit office using the VA Facility Locator: https://www.benefits.va.gov/benefits/offices.asp. Additional information may be found at: http://www.benefits.va.gov/pension/aid_attendance_housebound.asp.

Automobile Allowance: Servicemembers and Veterans may be eligible for a one-time payment of not more than $21,058.69, beginning October 1, 2018, toward the purchase of an automobile or other conveyance if you have certain service-connected disabilities. To apply, contact a VA regional office at 1-800-827-1000 or the nearest VA health care facility, which may be located at: https://www.va.gov/directory/guide/home.asp.

Clothing Allowance: Any Veteran who has service-connected disabilities that require prosthetic or orthopedic appliances may receive clothing allowances. This allowance is also available to any Veteran whose service-connected skin condition requires prescribed medication that irreparably damages outer garments. To receive annual payment, you must establish eligibility by August 1st of the year for which you claim payment. To apply, contact the prosthetic representative at the nearest VA medical center located at: https://www.va.gov/directory/guide/division.asp?dnum=1&isFlash=0.

For information on current rates visit: https://www.benefits.va.gov/COMPENSATION/special_Benefit_Allowances_2018.asp.

Additional Benefits for Eligible Military Retirees: Concurrent Retirement and Disability Pay (CRDP) is a DoD program that allows some individuals to receive both military retired pay and VA disability compensation. Normally, such concurrent receipt is prohibited. Veterans do not need to apply for this benefit, as payment is coordinated between VA and the military pay center. To qualify for CRDP, Veterans must have a VA service-connected disability rating of 50 percent or greater, be eligible to receive retired pay, and:

- Retire from military service based on longevity, including Temporary Early Retirement Authority (TERA) retirees; **or**

- Retire due to disability with 20 or more years of service*; **or**
- Retire from National Guard or Reserve service with 20 or more qualifying years.

* For Veterans who retired due to disability with 20 or more years of service, CRDP is subject to an offset for the difference between retired pay based on disability and retired pay based on longevity.

Housing Grants for Disabled Veterans: Service members and Veterans with certain service-connected disabilities may be entitled to a housing grant from VA to help build a new specially adapted house, to adapt a home they already own, or buy a house and modify it to meet their disability-related requirements. Eligible Veterans or service members may now receive up to three uses of the grant, with the total dollar amount of the grants not to exceed the maximum allowable. Housing grant amounts may be adjusted Oct. 1st every year based on a cost-of-construction index. These adjustments will increase the grants amounts or leave them unchanged; grant amounts will not decrease. Previous grant recipients who had received assistance of less than the current maximum allowable may be eligible for an additional grant usage. To obtain general information about the Specially Adapted Housing program, visit: https://www.benefits.va.gov/homeloans/adaptedhousing.asp or call the program's local office of jurisdiction at 1-877-827-3702.

Specially Adapted Housing (SAH) Grant: VA may approve a grant of not more than 50 percent of the cost of building, buying, or adapting existing homes or paying to reduce indebtedness on a currently owned home that is being adapted, up to a maximum benefit amount of $85,645. In certain instances, the full grant amount may be applied toward remodeling costs. The SAH grant is available to certain Veterans and service members who are entitled to disability compensation due to the following:

1. Loss or loss of use of both lower extremities, which so affects the functions of balance or propulsion to preclude ambulating without the aid of braces, crutches, canes or a wheelchair.

2. Loss or loss of use of both upper extremities at or above the elbow.

3. Blindness in both eyes, having only light perception, plus loss or loss of use of one lower extremity.

4. Loss or loss of use of one lower extremity together with (a) residuals of organic disease or injury, or (b) the loss or loss of use

of one upper extremity which so affects the functions of balance or propulsion as 15 to preclude locomotion without the use of braces, canes, crutches or a wheelchair.

5. Severe burn injuries, which are defined as full thickness or sub-dermal burns that have resulted in contractures with limitation of motion of two or more extremities or of at least one extremity and the trunk.

6. The loss, or loss of use of one or more lower extremities due to service on or after Sept. 11, 2001, which so affects the functions of balance or propulsion as to preclude ambulating without the aid of braces, crutches, canes, or a wheelchair. The authority for this specific entitlement category expired Sept. 30, 2018. Note, the entitlement authority also has a cap of 30 for the year.

Note: The property may be located outside the United States, in a country or political subdivision which allows individuals to have or acquire a beneficial property interest, and in which the Secretary of Veteran Affairs, in his or her discretion, has determined that is reasonably practicable to provide assistance in acquiring specially adapted housing. For more information on SAH, visit: https://www.benefits.va.gov/homeloans/adaptedhousing.asp or call the program's local office of jurisdiction at 1-877-827-3702.

Special Home Adaptation (SHA) Grant: VA may approve a benefit amount up to a maximum of $17,130 for the cost of necessary adaptations to a service member's or Veteran's residence or to help him/her acquire a residence already adapted with special features for his/her disability, to purchase and adapt a home, or for adaptations to a family member's home in which he/she will reside. To be eligible for this grant, service members and Veterans must be entitled to compensation for permanent and total service-connected disability due to one of the following:

1. Blindness in both eyes with 20/200 acuity or less.

2. Anatomical loss or loss of use of both hands.

3. Severe burn injuries (see above).

4. Certain severe respiratory injuries.

Temporary Residence Adaptation (TRA): Eligible Veterans and service members who are temporarily residing in a home owned by a family member may also receive a TRA grant to help the Veteran or service member adapt the family member's home to meet his or her special needs. Those eligible for an $85,645 grant would be permitted to use up to $37,597, and those eligible for a $17,130 grant would be permitted to use up to $6,713. Under the Honoring America's Veterans and Caring for Camp LeJeune Families Act of 2012, TRA grant amounts do not count against SAH or SHA grant maximum amounts, starting Aug. 6, 2013. Grant amounts are adjusted annually Oct.1st based on a cost-of-construction index.

Supplemental Financing: Veterans and service members with available VA Home Loan Guaranty entitlement may also obtain a guaranteed loan to supplement the grant to acquire a specially adapted home. For more information on SAH, visit: http://www.benefits.va.gov/homeloans/sah.asp.

Vocational Rehabilitation and Employment (VR&E): VR&E, also referred to as the Chapter 31 program, provides services to eligible service members and Veterans with service-connected disabilities and an employment handicap to help them to prepare for, obtain, and maintain suitable employment. For Veterans and service members with service-connected disabilities so severe that they cannot immediately consider work, VR&E provides services to improve their ability to live as independently as possible. For additional information on VR&E benefits please visit: http://www.benefits.va.gov/vocrehab/index.asp.

VR&E Eligibility for Veterans: A Veteran must have a VA service connected disability rating of at least 20 percent and determined to have an employment handicap, or rated 10 percent and determined to have a serious employment handicap, and must be discharged or released from active military service under other than dishonorable conditions.

VR&E Eligibility: Service members are eligible to apply if they expect to receive an honorable discharge upon separation from active duty, obtain a memorandum rating of 20 percent or more from VA, or obtain a proposed Disability Evaluation System (DES) rating of 20 percent or more from VA, or obtain a referral to a Physical Evaluation Board (PEB) through the Integrated Disability Evaluation System (IDES).

VR&E Entitlement: A Vocational Rehabilitation Counselor (VRC) works with the Veteran to determine if an employment handicap exists. An employment handicap exists if a Veteran's service-connected disability impairs his/her ability to prepare for, obtain, and maintain suitable employment. After an entitlement decision is determined, the Veteran and VRC work together to develop an individualized rehabilitation plan. The individualized rehabilitation plan outlines the necessary rehabilitation services to be provided to the Veterans and service members that are wounded, ill, injured, or in the IDES program and can receive National Defense Authorization Act authorized entitlement to VR&E when automatic referral by their chain of command.

VR&E Services: Veterans work with a VRC to select one of the five tracks to employment based on their individualized needs. The Five Tracks to Employment provide greater emphasis on exploring employment options early in the rehabilitation planning process, better informed choices for the Veteran regarding occupational and employment options, faster access to employment for Veterans who have identifiable and transferable skills for direct placement into suitable employment, and an option for Veterans who are not able to work, but need assistance to lead a more independent life. If a program of training is selected, VA pays the cost of the approved training and services (except those coordinated through other providers) that are outlined in the Veteran's rehabilitation plan, including subsistence allowance.

The Five Tracks to Employment are: Reemployment with previous employer, Rapid access to employment, Self-employment, Employment through long-term services, and Independent living services.

Period of a Rehabilitation Program: The basic period of eligibility in which VR&E benefits may be used is 12 years from the latter of the following: 1) A Veteran's date of separation from active military service, or 2) The date VA first notified a Veteran that he/she has been granted a compensable service-connected disability. Veterans may be provided up to 48 months of full-time services or the part-time equivalent based on the extent of services needed to complete the rehabilitation program. Rehabilitation plans that provide services to achieve the maximum level of independence cannot exceed 24 months which may be extended in certain circumstances.

Employment Services: In partnership with the Department of Labor, VA provides support to Veterans and transitioning service members at all stages of their job search, including career advice, resume building, and access to employers who want to hire Veterans and military spouses.

Additional information and access to services are available at https://www.va.gov/careers-employment/.

VR&E also establishes partnerships with Federal, state, and private agencies that help facilitate direct placement of Veterans or service members into civilian careers. VR&E can assist with placement using the following resources:

On the Job Training (OJT) Program: Employers hire Veterans at an apprentice wage, and VR&E supplements the salary at the journey-man wage (up to the maximum amount allowable under OJT). As the Veterans progress through training, the employers begin to increase the salary until the Veterans reach journeyman level and the employers pay the-entire salary. VR&E may also pay for any necessary tools.

Non-Paid Work Experience (NPWE): The NPWE program provides eligible Veterans the opportunity to obtain training and practical job experience concurrently. This program is ideal for Veterans or service members who have a clearly established vocational goal and who learn easily in a hands-on environment. This program is also well suited for Veterans who are having difficulties obtaining employment due to lack of work experience. The NPWE program may be established in a federal, state, or local (i.e. city, town, school district) government agencies only. The employer may hire the Veteran at any point during the NPWE program.

Compensated Work Therapy (CWT): is a VA clinical vocational rehabilitation program. CWT staffs provide:
- Evidence-based and evidence informed vocational rehabilitation services.
- Partnerships with business, industry and government agencies to provide Veteran candidates for employment and Veteran labor.
- Employment supports to Veterans and employers.

CWT programs strive to maintain highly responsive long-term quality relationships with business, government agencies, and industry promoting employment opportunities for Veterans with physical and mental health challenges. CWT programs are located within all VA medical centers. Review the CWT Locations page to find site specifics. Many of our CWT programs are accredited by the Commission on Accreditation of Rehabilitation Facilities (CARF). CARF International is an independent accrediting body of health and human service providers. CARF accreditation confirms that CWT programs are committed to continuous quality improvement, accountability for its performance through outcomes evidence, and monitoring the satisfaction of the persons served.

Special Employer Incentive (SEI): The SEI program is for eligible Veterans who face challenges in obtaining employment. Veterans approved to participate in the SEI program are hired by participating employers and employment is expected to continue following successful completion of the program. Employers are provided this incentive to hire Veterans. If approved, the employer will receive reimbursement for up to 50 percent of the Veteran's salary during the SEI program, which can last up to six months.

VetSuccess on Campus (VSOC): The VSOC program aims to help Veterans, service members, and eligible dependents succeed through a coordinated delivery of on-campus benefits assistance and counseling, leading to successful completion of their education and preparing them to enter the labor market in viable careers. For additional information on the VSOC program please visit: http://www.benefits.va.gov/vocrehab/vsoc.asp.

Chapter 36 Education and Career Counseling: VA's Education and Career Counseling Program (Title 38 U.S.C. Chapter 36) offers a great opportunity for transitioning Veterans, service members, and dependents to get personalized counseling and support to guide their career paths, ensure the most effective use of their VA benefits, and help them achieve their goals. For additional information please visit: http://www.benefits.va.gov/VOCREHAB/edu_voc_counseling.asp. To apply for this program, visit: https://www.ebenefits.va.gov.

VA Pension: VA helps Veterans and their families cope with financial challenges by providing supplemental income through the Veterans Pension and Survivors Pension benefit programs. Payments are made to bring the Veteran's or Survivor's total income, including other retirement or Social Security income, to a level set by Congress. Unreimbursed medical expenses may reduce countable income for VA purposes.

Veterans Pension: Congress establishes the maximum annual Veterans Pension rates. Payments are reduced by the amount of countable income of the Veteran, spouse, and dependent children. When a Veteran without a spouse or a child is furnished nursing home or domiciliary care by VA, the pension is reduced to an amount not to exceed $90 per month after three calendar months of care. The reduction may be delayed if nursing-home care is continued to provide the Veteran with rehabilitation services. To apply for increased pension based on A&A or Housebound payments, write to the Pension Management Center that serves your state and provide medical evidence, such as a doctor's report, that validates the need for an increased benefit. For additional information on pension benefits please visit: https://www.benefits.va.gov/pension/.

Eligibility for Veterans Pension: Generally, a Veteran must have at least 90 days of active duty service, with at least one day during a VA-recognized wartime period to qualify for a VA pension. The 90-day active service requirement does not apply to Veterans discharged from the military due to a service-connected disability. Veterans who entered active duty after Sept. 7, 1980, generally must have served at least 24 months of the full period for which called or ordered to active duty (with some exceptions), with at least one day during a war time period. In addition to meeting minimum service requirement, low-income wartime Veterans may qualify for pension if they meet certain service, income and net worth limits set by law and are: Age 65 or older, OR permanently and totally disabled, OR a patient in a nursing home receiving skilled nursing care, OR receiving Social Security Disability Insurance, OR receiving Supplemental Security Income.

Yearly family income must be less than the amount set by Congress to qualify for the Veterans Pension benefit. Payments are made to bring the Veteran's total income, including other retirement or Social Security income, to a level set by Congress. Unreimbursed medical expenses may reduce countable income for VA purposes.

Note: Veterans may have to meet longer minimum periods of active duty if they entered active duty on or after Sept. 8, 1980, or, if they were officers who entered active duty on or after Oct. 16, 1981. The Veteran's discharge must have been under conditions other than dishonorable, and the disability must be for reasons other than the Veteran's own willful misconduct.

How to Apply for Veterans Pension: To apply for Veterans Pension, download and complete **VA Form 21P 527EZ**, *"Application for Pension"*. You can mail your application to the Pension Management Center (PMC) that serves your state. You may also visit your local regional benefit office and turn in your application for processing. You can locate your local regional benefit office using the VA Facility Locator. For additional information on pension benefits please visit http://www.benefits.va.gov/pension.

Aid and Attendance and Housebound Benefits (Special Monthly Pension): Veterans and survivors who are eligible for VA pension and require the aid and attendance of another person, or are housebound, maybe eligible for a higher maximum annual pension rate. These benefits are paid in addition to monthly pension, and they are not paid without eligibility to pension. Since aid and attendance and housebound allowances increase the pension amount, people who are not eligible for a basic pension due to excessive income may be eligible for pension at these increased rates. A Veteran or surviving spouse may not receive aid and attendance benefits and housebound benefits at the same time. For additional information on aid and attendance and housebound benefits including how to apply please visit: http://www.benefits.va.gov/pension/aid_attendance_housebound.asp.

Education and Training Benefits

Post–9/11 GI Bill: The Post-9/11 GI Bill is an education benefit program for service members and Veterans who served on active duty after Sept.10, 2001. Benefits are payable for training pursued on or after Aug. 1, 2009. No payments can be made under this program for training pursued before that date. For additional information on education and training opportunities please visit: http://www.benefits.va.gov/gibill/ or by calling 1-888-GI-BILL-1 (1-888-442-4551).

Post–9/11 GI Bill Eligibility: To be eligible, the service member or Veteran must serve at least 90 aggregate days on active duty after Sept. 10, 2001, and remain on active duty or be honorably discharged. Active duty includes active service performed by National Guard members under title 32 U.S.C. for the purposes of organizing, administering, recruiting, instructing, or training the National Guard; or under section 502(f) for the purpose of responding to a national emergency. Veterans may also be eligible if they were honorably discharged from active duty for a service-connected disability after serving 30 continuous days after Sept. 10, 2001. Additionally, under the Colmery Act of 2017, also known as the "Forever GI Bill," all Purple Heart award recipients are eligible for Post 9/11 GI Bill entitlement providing the award was made during service occurring on or after Sept. 11, 2001, and the recipient continues on duty or receives an honorable discharge.

Contents of Benefit: Generally, service members or eligible Veterans may receive up to 36 months of entitlement under the Post-9/11 GI Bill. Based on the length of active duty service, eligible participants are entitled to receive a percentage of the cost of in-state tuition and fees at public institutions or the tuition and fees capped at a national maximum rate for private or foreign schools. Current rates can be found at http://www. benefits. va.gov/GIBILL/resources/benefits_resources/rate_tables.asp. The percentages and corresponding service requirements are noted in the chart below.

Service requirements after 9/10/01, an individual must serve an aggregate of:	Payment Tiers Percentage
At least 36 months	100 percent
At least 30 continuous days on active duty and discharged due to a service connected disability	100 percent
At least 30 months, but less than 36 Months	90 percent
At least 24 months, but less than 30 Months	80 percent
**At least 18 months, but less than 24 Months	70 percent
**At least 12 months, but less than 18 Months	60 percent
At least 6 months, but less than 12 Months*	50 percent
At least 90 days, but less than 6 Months*	40 percent

**Excludes time in basic military training and/or skill training.

***The Colmery Act will change the required amount of service noted above, effective 08/01/2020, resulting in more generous percentage of eligibility for service less than 12 months.

If a service members or Veteran is eligible for the Montgomery GI Bill; the Montgomery GI Bill-Selected Reserve; or the Reserve Educational Assistance Program, and qualifies for the Post-9/11 GI Bill, an irrevocable election must be made to receive benefits under the Post-9/11 GI Bill. Inmost instances, once the election to receive benefits under the Post-9/11 GI Bill is made, the individual will no longer be eligible to receive benefits under the relinquished program.

Tuition and fees are paid to the institution on the student's behalf (2017/2018: $22,805.34 and 2018/2019: $23,671.94) as well as a monthly Housing Allowance (MHA) currently equal to the basic allowance for housing payable to a military E-5 with dependents, in the same ZIP code of the main campus of the primary school (paid directly to the Veteran, or eligible dependents) but pro-rated based on benefit level and rate of pursuit (e.g., full-time student, ¾-time student, etc.). Please note, however, that MHA is not payable to individuals enrolled in flight or correspondence training, to individuals while pursuing training at half time or less (regardless of the type of training), or to individuals while on active duty or their spouses.

However, effective Aug. 1, 2018, under the Colmery Act, the MHA will be calculated based on the ZIP code of the campus location where the student physically attends a majority of classes rather than the location of the main campus of the school.

Additional benefits under the Post-9/11 GI Bill include a yearly books and supplies stipend of up to $1,000 per year (paid directly to the service member, Veteran, or eligible dependents), and a one-time payment of $500 paid to certain individuals relocating from highly rural areas.

Approved training under the Post-9/11 GI Bill includes graduate and undergraduate degrees, vocational/technical training, on-the job and apprenticeship training, flight training, correspondence training, licensing and national testing programs, and tutorial assistance.

The Yellow Ribbon G.I. Bill Education Enhancement Program: The Yellow Ribbon Program allows institutions of higher learning (such as colleges, universities, and other degree-granting schools) in the United States to voluntarily enter into an agreement with VA to fund tuition and fees that exceed the amounts payable under the Post-9/11 GI Bill. The institution can contribute a specified dollar amount of those expenses, and VA will match the contribution, not to exceed 50 percent of the difference. To be eligible, the student must be a Veteran or a transfer-of-entitlement-eligible dependent child receiving benefit at the 100-percent benefit rate. It is not available to active-duty-service members or their spouses using transferred entitlement, regardless of benefit level, or Marine Gunnery Sergeant John David Fry Scholarship (Fry Scholarship) recipients. However the Colmery Act will expand the Yellow Ribbon Program, as of Aug. 1, 2018, to include individuals who were awarded a Purple Heart on or after Sept. 11, 2001, as well as Fry Scholarship recipients, and, as of Aug. 1, 2022, to include active-duty service members eligible at the 100-percent benefit level, and their spouses using transferred entitlement.

Marine Gunnery Sergeant John David Fry Scholarship Eligibility: The Fry Scholarship provides Post-9/11 GI Bill® benefits to the children and surviving spouses of service members who died in the line of duty after Sept. 10, 2001. Eligible beneficiaries attending school may receive up to 36 months of benefits at the 100-percent level. The Fry Scholarship includes full tuition and fees paid directly to the school for all public school in-state students. For those attending private or foreign schools, tuition and fees are capped at a statutory maximum amount per academic year. A monthly housing allowance and a books and supplies stipend are also paid to the student.

Surviving children who are eligible may begin an approved program of education before the age of 18. A child's marital status has no effect on eligibility. Eligible children are entitled to 36 months of benefits at the 100-percent level. If the qualifying parent's death occurred before Jan. 1, 2013, the child's eligibility ends on his or her 33rd birthday. If the qualifying parent's death occurred on or after Jan. 1, 2013, the child's eligibility never expires.

Surviving spouses who are eligible have no timeline on when they can use the benefit; however, a spouse will lose eligibility for this benefit upon remarriage.

Survivor's & Dependents' Educational Assistance (DEA): The DEA program offers education and training opportunities to eligible dependents of Veterans who are permanently and totally disabled due to a service-related condition or of Veterans who died while on active duty or as a result of a service-related condition. Eligible surviving dependents may be eligible for 45 months of degree and certificate courses, apprenticeship, and on-the-job training.

To be eligible, you must be the son, daughter, or spouse of:
- A Veteran who died or is permanently and totally disabled as the result of a service-connected disability. The disability must arise out of active service in the armed forces.
- A Veteran who died from any cause while such permanent and total service-connected disability was in existence.
- A service member missing in action or captured in line of duty by a hostile force.
- A service member forcibly detained or interned in line of duty by a foreign government or power.
- A service member who is hospitalized or receiving outpatient treatment for a service connected permanent and total disability and is likely to be discharged for that disability. This change is effective December 23, 2006.

Surviving spouses lose eligibility if they remarry before age 57 or are living with another person who has been recognized publicly as their spouse. They can regain eligibility if their remarriage ends by death or divorce or if they cease living with the person. Dependent children do not lose eligibility if the surviving spouse remarries.

Provisions of the Colmery Act of 2017 will limit the months of benefit entitlement under DEA to 36 months (instead of 45) if enrollment in an education program occurs after Aug. 1, 2018.

Visit https://www.benefits.va.gov/gibill/survivor_dependent_assistance.asp for more information.

Period of Eligibility: The period of eligibility for Veterans' spouses expires 10 years from either the date they become eligible or the date of the Veteran's death. Children generally must be between the ages of 18 and 26 to receive educational benefits. VA may grant extensions to both spouses and children. The period of eligibility for spouses of service members who died on active duty expires 20 years from the date of death. Spouses of service members who died during active duty whose 10-year eligibility period expired before Dec. 10, 2004 have 20 years from the date of death to use educational benefits.

Training Available: Benefits may be awarded for pursuit of associate, bachelor, or graduate degrees at colleges and universities; independent study; cooperative training; study abroad; certificate or diploma from business, technical, or vocational schools; apprenticeships; on-the-job training programs; farm cooperative courses; and preparatory courses for tests required or used for admission to an institution of higher learning or graduate school.

Benefits for correspondence courses under certain conditions are available to spouses only. Beneficiaries without high-school degrees can pursue secondary schooling, and those with a deficiency in a subject may receive tutorial assistance if enrolled half-time or more.

Special Benefits: Dependents over age 14 with physical or mental disabilities that impair their ability to pursue an education may receive specialized vocational or restorative training, including speech and voice correction, language retraining, lip reading, auditory training, Braille reading and writing, and similar programs. Certain disabled or surviving spouses are also eligible. For additional information on Survivors' &

Dependents' Educational Assistance (DEA) visit: http://www.benefits. va.gov/GIBILL/DEA.asp.

Montgomery GI Bill Active Duty (MGIB-AD): The MGIB-AD (Chapter 30) is an education benefit that provides up to 36 months of education benefits to eligible Veterans and service members for college degree and certificate programs, technical or vocational courses, flight training, apprenticeships or on-the-job training, high tech training, licensing and certification test, entrepreneurship training, certain entrance examinations, and correspondence courses. Remedial, deficiency, and refresher courses may be ap- proved under certain circumstances. Benefits generally expire 10 years after discharge. Current payment rates are available at https://benefits.va.gov/GIBILL/resources/benefits_resources/rates/ch30/ ch30rates100117.asp. A Veteran may be eligible for this benefit if he or she entered active duty after June 30, 1985, has an honorable discharge, did not decline MGIB in writing, and served three continuous years of active duty (or have an obligation to serve four years in the Selected Reserve after active duty service). There are exceptions for disability, re-entering active duty, and upgraded discharges. All participants must have a high school diploma, equivalency certificate, or have completed 12 hours toward a college degree before applying for benefits.

GI Bill Resident-Rate Requirements: Section 3679, title 38, United States Code, requires VA to disapprove programs of education for payment of benefits under the Post-9/11 GI Bill and Montgomery GI Bill-Active Duty at public Institutions of Higher Learning (IHLs) if the school charges qualifying Veterans and dependents tuition and fees in excess of the rate for resident students. To remain approved for VA's GI Bill programs, schools must charge in-state tuition and fee amounts to "covered individuals." A covered individual is defined as: A Veteran who lives in the state where the IHL is located (regardless of his/her formal state of residence) and enrolls in the school within three years of discharge from a period of active duty service of 90 days or more.

An individual using transferred benefits who lives in the state where the IHL is located (regardless of his/her formal state of residence) and enrolls in the school within three years of the transferor's discharge from a period of active duty service of 90 days or more.

- Anyone described above while he or she remains continuously enrolled (other than during regularly scheduled breaks between courses, semesters, or terms) at the same school. The person so described must have enrolled in the school prior to the expiration of the three-year period following discharge or release as described above and must be using educational benefits under either chapter 30 or chapter 33, of title 38, United States Code.

- Anyone using transferred Post-9/11 GI Bill benefits who lives in the state where the IHL is located and the transferor is a member of the uniformed service who is serving on active duty.

- Anyone using benefits under the Marine Gunnery Sergeant John David Fry Scholarship who lives in the state where the IHL is located (regardless of his/her formal state of residence).

- The in-state tuition provisions do not apply to those individuals on active duty using benefits under the Post-9/11 GI Bill and Montgomery GI Bill-Active Duty.

Home Loan Guaranty: VA home loan guaranties are issued to help eligible service members, Veterans, Reservists, National Guard members, and certain surviving spouses obtain homes, condominiums, and manufactured homes, and to refinance loans.

Home Loan Guaranty Uses: A VA loan guaranty helps protect lenders from loss if the borrower fails to repay the loan. It can be used to obtain a loan to: buy an existing dwelling or build a home; buy a residential condominium unit; repair, alter, or improve a residence owned and occupied by the Veteran; refinance an existing home loan; buy a manufactured home and/or lot and install a solar heating or cooling system or other energy-efficient improvements.

Home Loan Guaranty Eligibility: Eligibility applications can be submitted electronically through eBenefits (www.ebenefits.va.gov) or by going through your lender, who will use the Automated Certificate of Eligibility system.

Although it's preferable for lenders and Veterans to apply electronically due to a majority of these requests being approved instantaneously by the eligibility system, it is possible to apply for a Certificate of Eligibility (COE) using VA Form 26-1880, Request for Certificate of Eligibility. Please note that while VA's electronic applications can establish eligibility and issue an online COE in a matter of seconds, the system can only process cases for which VA has sufficient data in its records. Therefore, certain applicants will not be able to establish eligibility online and additional information might be requested prior to the issuance of a COE. If a COE cannot be issued immediately, users have the option of submitting a hardcopy application. If applying manually for a COE using VA Form 26-1880, it is typically necessary that the eligible Veteran to present a copy of his/her report of discharge or DD Form 214, Certificate of Release or Discharge from Active Duty, or other adequate substitute evidence to VA, and be aware that it could take more time to process requests in this manner. An eligible active duty service member should obtain and submit a statement of service signed by an appropriate military official to the appropriate Regional Loan Center mentioned on VA Form 26-1880. For general program information or to obtain VA loan guaranty forms please visit http://www.benefits.va.gov/homeloans/ or call 1-877-827-3702 to reach the home loan program's local office of jurisdiction.

A completed VA Form 26-1880 and any associated documentation should be mailed to the nearest Regional Loan Center (RLC) of jurisdiction. The RLC jurisdictions and mailing addresses are located on page 3 of VA Form 26-1880, http://www.vba.va.gov/pubs/forms/vba-26-1880-are.pdf.

Credit and Income Qualifications: In addition to the periods of eligibility and conditions of service requirements, applicants must have sufficient income and credit, and agree to live in the property in order to be approved by a lender for a VA home loan.

Surviving Spouses: Some spouses of Veterans may have home loan eligibility: The unmarried surviving spouse of a Veteran who died as a result of service or service-connected causes; The surviving spouse of a Veteran who dies on active duty or from service connected causes, who remarries on or after attaining age 57 and on or after December 16, 2003; The spouse of an active duty member who is listed as missing in action (MIA) or a prisoner of war (POW) for at least 90 days.

Eligibility under the MIA/POW: Provisions are limited to one-time use only. Surviving spouses of Veterans who died from nonservice-connected causes may also be eligible if any of the following conditions are met: The Veteran was rated totally service-connected disabled for 10 years or more immediately preceding death, or was rated totally disabled for not less than five years from date of discharge or release from active duty to date of death, or was a former prisoner of war who died after Sept. 30, 1999, and was rated totally service connected disabled for not less than one year immediately preceding death.

Home Loan Guaranty Limits: VA does not make loans to Veterans and service members; VA guarantees loans made by private sector lenders. The guaranty is what VA could pay a lender should the loan go to fore-closure. VA does not set a cap on how much an individual can borrow to refinance a home. However, there are limits on the amount of liability VA can assume, which usually affects the amount of money an institution will lend. For information on loan limits please visit: http://www.benefits.gov/homeloans/purchaseco_loan_limits.asp.

Other Types of Loans: An eligible borrower can use a VA-guaranteed Interest Rate Reduction Refinancing Loan to refinance an existing VA loan and lower the interest rate and payment. Typically, no credit underwriting is required for this type of loan. The loan may include the entire outstand-ing balance of the prior loan, the costs of energy-efficient improvements, and closing costs, including up to two discounts points. An eligible bor-rower who wishes to obtain a VA-guaranteed loan to purchase a manu-factured home or lot can borrow up to 95 percent of the home's purchase price. The amount VA will guarantee on a manufactured home loan is 40 percent of the loan amount or the Veteran's available entitlement, up to a maximum amount of $20,000. These provisions apply only to a manufac-tured home that will not be placed on a permanent foundation.

Home Loan Guaranty Appraisals: In most cases, a home loan cannot be guaranteed by VA without first being appraised by a VA-assigned fee appraiser. A home appraisal by a VA-assigned fee appraiser is required for purchase and certain refinance loans guaranteed by VA. A lender can request a VA appraisal through VA systems. The Veteran borrower typi-cally pays for the appraisal upon completion, according to a fee schedule approved by VA. This VA appraisal estimates the value of the property. An appraisal is not an inspection and does not guarantee the house is free of defects. VA guarantees the loan, not the condition of the property.

A thorough inspection of the property by a reputable inspection firm may help minimize any problems that could arise after loan closing. In an existing home, particular attention should be given to plumbing, heating, electrical, roofing, and structural components. In addition, VA strongly recommends testing for radon, a known carcinogen.

Home Loan Guaranty Closing Costs: For purchase home loans, pay-ment in cash is required on all closing costs, including title search and recording fees, hazard insurance premiums, and prepaid taxes. For refi-nancing loans, all such costs may be included in the loan, as long as the total loan does not exceed the reasonable value of the property. Interest rate reduction loans may include closing costs, including a maximum of two discount points.

Home Loan Guaranty Funding Fees: The funding fee is a percentage of the loan amount collected in order to offset future anticipated costs associated with the loan. A funding fee must be paid to VA unless the Veteran is exempt from such a fee. Currently, exemptions from the funding fee are provided for Veterans and service members receiving VA disability compensation, those who are rated by VA as eligible to receive compensation as a result of pre-discharge disability examination and rating, and those who would be in receipt of compensation, but who were recalled to active duty or reenlisted and are receiving active-duty pay in lieu of compensation. Additionally, unmarried surviving spouses in receipt of dependency and indemnity compensation may be exempt. The fee may be paid in cash or included in the loan. For all types of loans, the loan amount may include the VA funding fee and up to **$6,000** of energy-efficient improvements.

However, no other fees including fees for the VA appraisal, credit report, loan processing fee, title search, title insurance, recording fees, transfer taxes, survey charges, or hazard insurance charges, or discount points may be included in loans for purchase or construction. For refinancing loans, most closing costs may be included in the loan amount.

Home Loan Guaranty Required Occupancy: To qualify for a VA home loan, a Veteran or the spouse of an active-duty service member must certify that he or she intends to occupy the home. A dependent child of an active-duty service member also satisfies the occupancy requirement. When refinancing a VA-guaranteed loan solely to reduce the interest rate, a Veteran only needs to certify prior occupancy.

Home Loan Guaranty Financing, Interest Rates and Terms: Veterans obtain VA-guaranteed loans through the usual lending institutions, including banks, credit unions, and mortgage brokers. VA-guaranteed loans can have either a fixed interest rate or an adjustable rate, where the interest rate may adjust up to 1 percent annually and up to 5 percent over the life of the loan. VA does not set the interest rate. Interest rates are negotiable between the lender and borrower on all loan types.

Veterans may also choose a different type of adjustable rate mortgage called a hybrid ARM, where the initial interest rate remains fixed for 3-10 years. If the rate remains fixed for less than five years, the rate adjustment cannot be more than 1 percent annually and 5 percent over the life of the loan. For a hybrid ARM with an initial fixed period of five years or more, the initial adjustment may be up to 2 percent.

The Secretary has the authority to determine annual adjustments thereafter. Currently, annual adjustments may be up to 2 percentage point and 6 percent over the life of the loan. If the lender charges discounts points on the loan, the Veteran may negotiate with the seller as to who will pay points or if they will be split between buyer and seller. Points paid by the Veteran may not be included in the loan (with the exception that up to two points may be included in interest rate reduction refinancing loans). The term of the loan may be for as long as 30 years and 32 days.

Home Loan Guaranty Assumption Requirements and Liability: VA loans made on or after March 1, 1988, are not assumable without the prior approval of VA or its authorized agent (usually the lender collecting the monthly payments). To approve the assumption, the lender must ensure that the purchaser is a satisfactory credit risk and will assume all of the Veteran's liabilities on the loan. If approved, the purchaser will have to pay a funding fee that the lender sends to VA, and the Veteran will be released from liability to the federal government. (A VA-guaranteed loan may be assumed by Veterans, active duty personnel, and non-Veterans alike.)

Loans made prior to March 1, 1988, are generally freely assumable, but Veterans should still request the lender's approval in order to be released of liability. Veterans whose loans were closed after December 31, 1989, usually have no liability to the government following a foreclosure, except in cases involving fraud, misrepresentation, or bad faith, such as allowing an unapproved assumption. However, for the entitlement to be restored, any loss suffered by VA must be paid in full.

A release of liability does not mean that a Veteran's guaranty entitlement is restored. That occurs only if the borrower is an eligible Veteran who agrees to substitute his or her entitlement for that of the seller. If the Veteran allows assumptions of a loan without prior approval, then the lender may demand immediate and full payment of the loan, and the Veteran may be liable if the loan is foreclosed and VA has to pay a claim under the loan guaranty.

VA Assistance to Veterans in Default: When a VA-guaranteed home loan becomes delinquent, VA may provide supplemental servicing assistance to help cure the default. The servicer has the primary responsibility of servicing the loan to resolve the default, and VA urges all Veterans who are encountering problems making their mortgage payments to speak with their servicers as soon as possible to explore options to avoid fore-closure. Contrary to popular opinion, servicers do not want to foreclose, because foreclosure costs money. Depending on a Veteran's specific situa-tion, servicers may offer any of the following options to avoid foreclosure:

- **Repayment Plan** – the borrower makes a regular installment each month plus part of the missed installments.
- **Special Forbearance** – the servicer agrees not to initiate foreclo-sure to allow time for borrowers to repay the missed installments or agrees to place a hold or postpone foreclosures proceedings. An example of when this would be likely is when a borrower is waiting for a tax refund.
- **Loan Modification** – provides the borrower a fresh start by adding the delinquency to the loan balance and establishing a new payment schedule.
- **Short Sale** – when the servicer agrees to allow a borrower to sell his/her home for a lesser amount than what is currently required to pay off the loan.
- **Deed-in-Lieu of Foreclosure** – the borrower voluntarily agrees to deed the property to the servicer instead of going through a lengthy foreclosure process. In cases where the servicer is unable to help the Veteran borrower, VA has loan technicians at its eight RLCs and in Hawaii, who are available to take an active role in interceding with the mortgage servicer. Veterans with VA-guaranteed home loans can call 1-877-827-3702 to discuss potential ways to help save the loan.

Service Members Civil Relief Act (SCRA) and Home Loan Guaranties: Veteran borrowers may be able to request relief pursuant to the SCRA. In order to qualify for certain protections available under the Act, their obli-gation must have originated prior to their current period of active military service. SCRA may provide a lower interest rate during military service and for up to one year after service ends, provide forbearance, or prevent foreclosure or eviction up to nine months from period of military service.

Assistance to Veterans with VA-Guaranteed Home Loans: When a VA-guaranteed home loan becomes delinquent, VA may provide supple-mental servicing assistance to help cure the default. The servicer has the primary responsibility of servicing the loan to resolve the default.

Veterans with VA-guaranteed home loans can call **1-877-827-3702** to reach the nearest VA office where loan specialists are prepared to discuss potential ways to help save the loan.

Assistance to Veterans with Non-VA Guaranteed Home Loans in Default: VA advises Veterans or service members who are having difficulty making payments on a non-VA-guaranteed loan to contact their servicer as quickly as possible to explore options to avoid foreclosure. Although for non-VA loans, VA does not have authority to directly intervene on the borrower's behalf, VA's network of loan technicians at eight Regional Loan Centers and an office in Hawaii can offer advice and guidance on how to potentially avoid foreclosure. Veterans or service members with non-VA loans may call **1-877-827-3702** to speak with a VA loan technician, or visit: http://www.benefits.va.gov/homeloans/, for more information on avoiding foreclosure.

If VA is not able to help a Veteran borrower retain his/her home (whether a VA-guaranteed loan or not), the Department of Housing and Urban Development (HUD) offers assistance to homeowners by sponsoring local housing counseling agencies. To find an approved agency in your area, search online at https://apps.hud.gov/offices/hsg/sfh/hcc/hcs.cfm or call HUD's interactive voice system at 1-**800-569-4287**.

VA Refinancing of a Non-VA Guaranteed Home Loan: Veterans with non-VA guaranteed home loans now have new options for refinancing to a VA-guaranteed home loan. These new options are available as a result of the Veterans' Benefits Improvement Act of 2008. Veterans who wish to refinance their subprime or conventional mortgage may now do so for up to 100 percent of value of the property.

Other Assistance for Delinquent Veteran Borrowers: If VA is not able to help a Veteran borrower retain his/her home (whether a VA-guaranteed loan or not), the Department of Housing and Urban Development (HUD) offers assistance to homeowners by sponsoring local housing counseling agencies. To find an approved agency in your area, please visit: http://www.hud.gov/offices/hsg/sfh/hcc/hcs.cfm or call HUD's interactive voice system at **1-800-569-4287**.

Preventing Veteran Homelessness: Veterans who believe they may be facing homelessness as a result of losing their homes can call 1-877-4AID-VET (877-424-3838) or visit: https://www.va.gov/homeless/ to receive assistance in preventing homelessness.

VA Acquired Property Sales: VA acquires properties as a result of fore-closures of VA-guaranteed and VA-owned loans. A private contractor currently markets the acquired properties through listing agents using local Multiple Listing Services. A listing of "VA Properties for Sale" may be found at http://listings.vrmco.com/. Contact a real estate agent for information on purchasing a VA-acquired property.

Loans for Native American Veterans: Eligible Native American Veterans can obtain a loan from VA to purchase, construct, or improve a home on federal Trust Land, or to reduce the interest rate on such a VA loan. Native American Direct Loans (NADL) are only available if a memorandum of understanding exists between the tribal organization and VA. Veterans who are not Native American, but who are married to Native American non-Veterans, may be eligible for a direct loan under this program. To be eligible for such a loan, the qualified non-Native American Veteran and the Native American spouse must reside on federal Trust Land, both the Veteran and spouse must have a meaningful interest in the dwelling or lot, and the tribal authority that has jurisdiction over the Trust Land must recognize the non-Native American Veteran as subject to its authority. For additional information about the NADL program please visit: http://www.benefits.va.gov/homeloans/nadl.asp.

VA Life Insurance: VA's life insurance benefits open to new applicants include Service members' Group Life Insurance, Veterans' Group Life Insurance, Family Service members' Group Life Insurance, Service members' Group Life Insurance Traumatic Injury Protection, Service-Disabled Veterans' Insurance, and Veterans' Mortgage Life Insurance.

These programs are described below. Complete details are also available at: http://www.benefits.va.gov/insurance/; or by writing to Department of Veterans Affairs, Insurance Center, P.O. Box 42954, Philadelphia, PA 19101or by calling VA's Insurance Center toll-free at **1-800-669-8477.** Specialists are available between the hours of 8:30 a.m. and 6:00 p.m. (EST) Monday through Friday to discuss: eligibility, premium payments, insurance dividends, address changes, policy loans, naming beneficiaries, reporting the death of the insured and other insurance issues.

For information about Service Members' Group Life Insurance, Veterans' Group Life Insurance, Service Members' Group Life Insurance Traumatic Injury Protection or Family Service Members' Group Life Insurance coverage, please visit: http://www.benefits.va.gov/insurance/; or call the Office of Service Members' Group Life Insurance directly at **1-800-419-1473**.

Service Members'Group Life Insurance (SGLI): The following persons are automatically insured by law for $400,000 under SGLI:

- Active-duty members of the Army, Navy, Air Force, Marines and Coast Guard

- Commissioned members of the National Oceanic and Atmospheric Administration (NOAA)

- U.S. Public Health Service (UPHS)

- Cadets or midshipmen of the U.S. military academies

- Members, cadets and midshipmen of the Reserved Officers Training Corps (ROTC) while engaged in authorized training and practice cruises

- Members of the Ready Reserves/National Guard who are scheduled to perform at least 12 periods of inactive training per year

- Service members who volunteer for a mobilization category in the Individual Ready Reserve (IRR)

Individuals may elect in writing to be covered for less than $400,000 or to decline coverage. SGLI coverage is available in $50,000 increments up to the maximum of $400,000. Full-time service members on active duty are covered 24 hours a day, 7 days a week for 365 days of the year.

Full-time SGLI Coverage: Full-time coverage is in effect during periods of active duty and for Ready Reserve and National Guard members scheduled to perform at least 12 periods of inactive duty training per year. Coverage is also provided for 120 days after separation or release from duty for service members who quality for full-time SGLI coverage. Reservists or National Guard members who have been assigned to a unit in which they are scheduled to perform at least 12 periods of inactive duty that is creditable for retirement purposes are also covered 24 hours a day, 7 days a week for 365 days of the year and for 120 days following separation or release from duty.

Part-time SGLI Coverage: Part-time coverage is provided for Reservists or National Guard members who do not qualify for the full-time coverage described above. Part-time coverage generally applies to Reservists/ National Guard members who drill only a few days in a year. These individuals are covered only while on active duty or active duty for training, or while traveling to and from such duty. Members covered part time do not receive 120 days of free coverage after separation unless they incur or aggravate a disability during a period of duty. For additional information about SGLI coverage, please visit: https://www.benefits.va.gov/insurance/sgli.asp.

SGLI Traumatic Injury Protection (TSGLI): Members of the armed services serve our nation heroically during times of great need, but what happens when they experience great needs of their own because they have sustained a traumatic injury? TSGLI provides payment to traumatically injured service members who have suffered certain physical losses. The TSGLI benefit ranges between $25,000 and $100,000 depending on the loss suffered. TSGLI helps service members by providing financial resources that allow their families to be with them during their recovery or by helping them with other expenses incurred during their recovery period.

TSGLI is part of SGLI. An additional $1 is added to the service member's SGLI premium to cover TSGLI. After Dec. 1, 2005, all service members who are covered by SGLI are automatically also covered by TSGLI. TSGLI cannot be declined unless the service member also declines basic SGLI. TSGLI claims are adjudicated by the service members military branches of service. In addition, there is retroactive TSGLI coverage for service members who sustained a qualifying loss between Oct. 7, 2001 and Nov. 30, 2005 regardless of where it occurred; TSGLI coverage is also payable to these service members regardless of whether they had SGLI coverage in force at the time of their injury.

For additional information about TSGLI eligibility and branch of service contact information, please visit: http://benefits.va.gov/insurance/tsgli. asp, or call:

1-800-237-1336 (Army);

1-866-827-5672, option2 (Navy);

1-877-216-0825 or 1-703-432-9277 (Marine Corps);

1-800-433-0048 (Active Duty Air Force);

1-800-525-0102 (Air Force Reserves);

1-240-612-9151 (Air National Guard); 1-202-795-6647 (Coast Guard);

1-301-427-3280 (Public Health Service);

1-301-713-3444 (National Oceanic and Atmospheric Administration)

Family Service Members' Group Life Insurance Coverage (FSGLI):
FSGLI coverage consists of spousal coverage and dependent child coverage. FSGLI provides term life insurance coverage for the spouse and dependent children of service members insured under **SGLI**. The service member must pay a premium for spousal coverage. Dependent children are insured at no cost to the service member. Family coverage is available only to service members insured under the SGLI program, not Veterans' Group Life Insurance (**VGLI**).

Spousal Coverage*: FSGLI provides up to $100,000 of life insurance coverage for a spouse of a service member with full-time SGLI coverage, which can not to exceed the amount of SGLI the service member has in force. Coverage for spouses who are not in the military is automatic.

For spouses who are in the military at the same time as the SGLI insured service member and who got married on or after Jan. 2, 2013, coverage is not automatic. The service members in this category must apply for spousal coverage for their military spouse, and their spouses must meet good health requirements. Premiums for spousal coverage are based on the age of the spouse and the amount of FSGLI coverage. FSGLI is a service members' benefit; the member pays the premium and is the only person allowed to be the beneficiary of the coverage.

FSGLI spousal coverage ends due to any of the following events:

- The service member elects in writing to terminate his or her own SGLI coverage.
- The service member elects in writing to terminate FSGLI coverage on his or her spouse.
- The service member divorces his or her spouse.
- The insured service member dies.
- The service member separates from service.

*The insured spouse may convert his or her FSGLI coverage to a permanent policy offered by participating private insurers within 120 days of the date of any of the termination events noted above.

SGLI Online Enrollment System (SOES): If a service member is in the Navy, Air Force or Army spousal coverage under Service Members' Group Life Insurance (SGLI) coverage can now be managed using the SGLI

Online Enrollment System (SOES). SOES allows service members with full-time SGLI coverage to make changes to their life insurance coverage and beneficiary information online at any time without completing a paper form or making a trip to their personnel office. To access SOES, the service member must sign into the MilConnect portal at https://milconnect.dmdc.osd.mil/milconnect/ and go to the *Benefits Tab, Life Insurance SOES-SGLI Online Enrollment System*.

Service members in branches other than the *Navy, Air Force* or *Army* must complete and submit the SGLI Form **SGLV 8286A,** *Family Coverage Election, service members' Group Life Insurance* to change their FSGLI spousal coverage elections. The service member should contact their Personnel Office for any changes to Basic SGLI, Family SGLI coverage, or **to find out when their service is scheduled to begin using SOES**.

Dependent Child Coverage: FSGLI dependent coverage of $10,000 is also automatically provided for dependent children of service members insured under SGLI, with no premium required. FSGLI Dependent Child coverage cannot be declined. FSGLI Dependent Child coverage ends when one of the following events occurs:

- The service member elects in writing to decline SGLI coverage

- The child(ren) no longer qualifies as an insurable dependent as defined by 38 U.S.C. 1965

- The service member dies

- The service member is discharged from the service

Dependent child coverage cannot be converted to a commercial policy.

For additional information about FSGLI coverage, please visit: https://www.benefits.va.gov/insurance/fsgli.asp.

Veterans' Group Life Insurance (VGLI): VGLI is lifetime renewable term coverage available to former service members who had SGLI at the time of separation which includes the following persons.

- Former service members who had full-time SGLI coverage upon separation from active duty or the Reserves

- Former service members of the Ready Reserves/National Guard with part-time SGLI coverage who incur a disability or aggravate a pre-existing disability during a period of active duty or a period of inactive duty for less than 31 days that renders them uninsurable at standard premium rates

- Former service members of the Individual Ready Reserve and Inactive National Guard

SGLI coverage may be converted to VGLI after separation from service. Former service members must apply for VGLI within one-year and 120 days from separation from service to qualify.

Service members separated from service on or after Nov. 1, 2012, who apply for VGLI within 240 days of separation, do not need to submit evidence of good health, while service members who apply after the 240-day period after separation must submit evidence of insurability. The initial VGLI coverage available is equal to the amount of SGLI coverage held at the time of separation from service unless the service member elects less VGLI coverage after separation.

Effective April 11, 2011, VGLI insureds who are under age 60 and have less than $400,000 in coverage can purchase up to $25,000 of additional coverage on each five-year anniversary of their initial coverage, up to the maximum $400,000. The option to purchase additional VGLI starts from the one-year anniversary of initial VGLI coverage date. The option to increase VGLI coverage thereafter is available every five years as long as the former service member meets the eligibility criteria. No medical underwriting is required for the additional coverage.

For additional information about VGLI coverage, please visit: https://www.benefits.va.gov/insurance/vgli.asp.

SGLI Disability Extension: Service members who are totally disabled at the time of separation (i.e. unable to work due to disabilities or have certain statutory conditions), can apply for the SGLI Disability Extension, which provides free coverage for up to two years from the date of separation. To apply, service members must complete and return **SGLV 8715**, the SGLI Disability Extension Application. Those covered under the SGLI Disability Extension are automatically converted to VGLI at the end of their extension period, subject to the payment of premiums. VGLI is convertible at any time to a permanent plan policy with any participating commercial insurance company.

For additional information about the SGLI coverage, please visit: https://www.benefits.va.gov/insurance/sglidisabled.asp.

Accelerated Death Benefits: Like many private life insurance companies, the SGLI, FSGLI and VGLI programs offer an accelerated benefits option to terminally ill insured members. An insured service member is considered to be terminally ill if he or she has a written medical prognosis of nine months or less to live. All terminally ill insureds are eligible to receive advance payment of up to 50 percent of their SGLI or VGLI coverage, and terminally ill spouses can receive up to 50 percent of their FSGLI in a lump sum. Payment of an accelerated benefit does however reduce the amount payable to the beneficiaries at the time of the insured's death.

To apply, an insured member must submit **SGLV 8284**, *Service member/ Veteran Accelerated Benefit Option form*, and spouses must complete **SGLV 8284A**, *Service member Family Coverage Accelerated Benefits Option form*.

For additional information about the Accelerated Benefit Option, please visit: https://www.benefits.va.gov/insurance/abo.asp.

Service-Disabled Veterans' Insurance (S-DVI): Veterans who separated from service on or after April 25, 1951, under other than dishonorable conditions who have VA rated service-connected disabilities, even disabilities that are 0-percent disabling, but are otherwise in good health, may apply to VA for up to $10,000 in life insurance coverage under the S-DVI program.

Applications must be submitted to the VA Insurance Center in Philadelphia *within* two years from the date of being notified of the approval of a new service-connected disability by VA. Veterans who are totally disabled (i.e. unable to work due to disability (ies) or have certain statutory conditions) may apply for a waiver of their S-DVI premiums. If approved for waiver of premiums, the Veteran can apply for additional supplemental S-DVI coverage of up to $30,000. However, premiums cannot be waived on the additional supplemental S-DVI.

To be eligible for this type of supplemental insurance, Veterans must meet all three requirements below:

1. be under age 65;

2. be eligible for a waiver of S-DVI premiums due to total disability; *and*

3. apply for additional insurance within one year from the date of notification of approval of waiver of premiums on the basic S-DVI policy.

For additional information about S-DVI and Supplemental S-DVI, please visit: https://www.benefits.va.gov/insurance/s-dvi.asp.

Veterans'Mortgage Life Insurance (VMLI): VMLI is mortgage protection insurance available to service members and Veterans under the age of 70 who have severe service-connected disabilities that qualify them for a SAH Grant from the VA Loan Guaranty Service. SAH Grants help severely disabled Veterans build, remodel or purchase a home.

Maximum VMLI coverage is the smaller of the existing mortgage balance or $200,000 and is payable only to the mortgage company upon the insured's death. To qualify for VMLI coverage, the service member or Veteran must the following elements:

1. qualify for the VA SAH grant for the home

2. have title to or ownership rights in the home, and

3. have a mortgage on the home

VMLI premiums are based on the age of the service member or Veteran, the length of the mortgage, the balance of the mortgage at the time of application and the amount of VMLI coverage requested; the service member/Veteran will need to provide this information to VA to determine the premium.

VMLI coverage automatically terminates when: 1) the mortgage is paid off in full; 2) the service member or Veteran terminates ownership in the property secured by the mortgage; 3) the service member or Veteran requests termination of coverage; 4) the service member or Veteran fails to provide required information (i.e. premiums or mortgage information); 5) the premium is not paid; or 6) the service member or Veteran dies.

If a mortgage is disposed of through sale of the property, VMLI may be obtained on the mortgage of another home.

For additional information about VMLI, please visit: https://www.benefits.va.gov/insurance/vmli.asp.

Other Insurance Information: The following information applies only to policies issued to World War II, Korean-era, Vietnam-era Veterans and persons with Service-Disabled Veterans' Insurance policies. Policies in this group are prefixed by the letters K, V, RS, W, J, JR, JS, or RH.

Insurance Dividends Issued Annually: World War II and Korean Era Veterans with active policies beginning with the letters V, RS, W, J, JR, JS, or K earn *tax-free dividends* annually on the policy anniversary date. (Policies prefixed by RH do not earn dividends.)

Policyholders do not need to apply for dividends, but may select among the following dividend options:

Cash: The dividend is paid directly to the insured by direct deposit to a bank account or by U.S. Treasury check.

Paid-Up Additional Insurance: The dividend is used to purchase additional insurance coverage for all policies except policy numbers that begin with the letter "K".

Credit or Deposit: The dividend is held in an account for the policyholder with interest. Withdrawals from the account can be made at any time. The interest rate may be adjusted. (There are, however, limitations regarding the dividend credit option for term insurance policies.)

Net Premium Billing Options: These options use the dividend to pay the annual policy premium. If the dividend exceeds the premium, the policyholder has options to choose how the remainder is used. If the dividend is not enough to pay an annual premium, the policyholder is billed the balance.

Other Dividend Options: Dividends can also be used to repay a policy loan or pay premiums in advance.

Reinstating Lapsed Insurance: *Lapsed term policies* may be reinstated within five years from the date of lapse. A five-year term policy that is not lapsed at the end of the term is automatically renewed for an additional five years. *Lapsed permanent plans* may be reinstated within certain time limits and with certain health requirements. Reinstated permanent plan policies require repayment of all back premiums, plus interest.

Converting Term Policies: Term policies are renewed automatically every five years, with premiums increasing at each renewal. Premiums do not increase after age 70. Term policies may be converted to permanent plans, which have fixed premiums for life and earn cash and loan values.

Dividends on Capped Term Policies: Effective Sept. 11, 2000, VA provides either a cash dividend or paid-up insurance on term policies whose premiums have been capped. Veterans with National Service Life Insurance (NSLI) term insurance that has renewed at age 71 or older and who stop paying premiums on their policies will be given a "termination dividend".

This dividend can either be received as a cash payment or used to purchase a reduced amount of paid-up insurance, which insures the Veteran for life with no premium payments required. The amount of the reduced paid-up insurance remains level. This does not apply to S-DVI (RH) policies.

Borrowing on Policies: Policyholders with permanent plan policies may borrow up to 94 percent of the cash surrender value of their insurance after the insurance is in force for one year or more. Interest is compounded annually. The loan interest rate is variable and may be obtained by calling toll-free at **1-800-669-8477**.

Reserve and National Guard Re-Employment Rights: A person who left a civilian job to enter active duty in the armed forces is entitled to return to the job after discharge or release from active duty if they:

- gave advance notice of military service to the employer;

- did not exceed five years' cumulative absence from the civilian job (with some exceptions);

- submitted a timely application for re-employment; and

- did not receive a dishonorable or other punitive discharge.

The law calls for a returning Veteran to be placed in the job as if he/she had never left, including benefits based on seniority such as pensions, pay increases and promotions. The law also prohibits discrimination in hiring, promotion, or other advantages of employment on the basis of military service. Veterans seeking re-employment should apply, verbally or in writing, to the company's hiring official and keep a record of their application. If problems arise, contact the Department of Labor's Veterans' Employment and Training Service (VETS) in the state of the employer. Federal employees not properly re-employed may appeal directly to the Merit Systems Protection Board. Non-federal employees may file complaints in U.S. District Court. For information, visit https://www.dol.gov/agencies/vets/programs/userra.

Special Groups of Veterans

Veterans and Survivors Needing Fiduciary Services: The fiduciary program provides oversight of VA's most vulnerable beneficiaries who are unable to manage their VA benefits because of injury, disease, the infirmities of advanced age, or being under 18 years of age. VA closely monitors fiduciaries for compliance with program responsibilities to ensure that VA benefits are being used for the purpose of meeting the needs, security, and comfort of beneficiaries and their dependents. In deciding who should act as fiduciary for a beneficiary, VA will always select the most effective and least restrictive fiduciary arrangement. For more information about VA's fiduciary program, please visit our website at https://benefits. va.gov/fiduciary/index.asp.

Homeless Veterans: VA's homeless programs constitute the largest integrated network of homeless assistance programs in the country, offering a wide array of services to help Veterans recover from homelessness and live as self-sufficiently and independently as possible. For more information on VA homeless programs and services, Veterans currently enrolled in VA health care can speak with their VA mental health or health care provider. Other Veterans and interested parties can find a complete list of VA health care facilities at https://www.va.gov/find-locations/?facilityType=health, or they can call VA's general information hotline at 1-800-827-1000. If assistance is needed when contacting a VA facility, ask to speak to the Health Care for Homeless Veterans Program or the Mental Health service manager. For additional information please visit: http://www.benefits.va.gov/PERSONA/veteran-homeless.asp or call VA's National Call Center for Homeless Veterans at 1-888 AIDVET (1-888-424-3838).

Homeless Veterans Dental Program: The Homeless Veterans Dental Program was established by the Veterans Administration in 1992. The program is funded through the Office of Dentistry and located at the James A. Haley Veterans' Hospital. For additional information on the Homeless Dental Program please visit: https://www.va.gov/homeless/dental.asp.

VA Health Care for Homeless Veterans (HCHV) Program: The HCHV Program provides a gateway to VA and community supportive services for eligible Veterans. Through the HCHV Program, Veterans are provided with case management and residential treatment in the community. The program also conducts outreach to homeless Veterans who are not likely to come to VA facilities on their own. For more information on VA homeless programs and services, Veterans currently enrolled in VA health care can speak with their VA mental health or health care provider. Other Veterans and interested parties can find a complete list of VA health care facilities at http://www.va.gov, or they can call VA's general information hotline at **1-800-827-1000**. If assistance is needed when contacting a VA facility, ask to speak to the Health Care for Homeless Veterans Program or the Mental Health service manager. For additional information on VA Homeless program website please visit: https://www.va.gov/homeless/.

Homeless Veteran Community Employment Services (HVCES): The HVCES Program provides a range of site-specific employment services rather than being a discrete program. There are no eligibility requirements for Veterans to receive assistance from HVCES other than participation in a VHA homeless program.

HVCES staff ensure a range of employment services are accessible to Veterans who have experienced homelessness. Individualized employment services are provided to overcome barriers preventing the Veteran from returning to work, such as a poor work history, lack of transportation and appropriate clothing, history of justice involvement and co-occurring substance use and/or mental health issues.

HVCES staff, embedded in homeless programs within the medical centers, complement existing medical center-based employment services, and are a bridge to employment opportunities and resources in the local community. HVCES is staffed by community employment coordinators (CECs), located at each VA medical center, and employment specialists within the Health Care for Homeless Veterans (HCHV) and Department of Housing and Urban Development-VA Supportive Housing (HUD-VASH) Programs, who are located at a limited number of VA medical centers. For more information about HVCES, please visit: https://www.va.gov/HOMELESS/HVCES.asp.

Homeless Providers Grant and Per Diem Program (GPD): The GPD Program is offered annually (as funding permits) by the Department of Veterans Affairs Health Care for Homeless Veterans (HCHV) Programs to fund non-profit community agencies that provide services to homeless Veterans. The purpose of the program is to promote the development and provision of supportive housing and/or supportive services with the goal of helping homeless Veterans achieve residential stability, increase their skill levels and/or income, and obtain greater self-determination.

Only programs with supportive housing (up to 24 months) or service centers (offering services such as case management, education, crisis intervention, counseling, services targeted towards specialized populations including homeless women Veterans, etc.) are eligible for these funds.

For more information, visit: http://www.va.gov/homeless/gpd.asp.

Housing and Urban Development-Veterans Affairs Supportive Housing (HUD-VASH) Program: The HUD-VASH Program provides permanent housing and case management for eligible homeless Veterans who need community-based support to secure and keep stable housing. This program allows eligible Veterans to live in Veteran selected housing units with a "Housing Choice" voucher. These vouchers are portable to support the Veteran's choice of housing in communities served by their VA medical facility where case management services can be provided. For more information, please visit: www.va.gov/homeless/hud-vash.asp.

Supportive Services for Veterans Families (SSVF) Program: The SSVF Program is designed to rapidly re-house homeless Veteran families and prevent homelessness for those at imminent risk due to a housing crisis. Funds are granted to private non-profit organizations and consumer cooperatives that will assist very low-income Veteran families by providing a range of supportive services designed to promote housing stability. To locate a SSVF provider in your community, please visit: http://www.va.gov/homeless/ssvf.asp and look for the list of current year SSVF providers or call VA's National Call Center for Homeless Veterans at **1-888-4AID-VET (1-888-424-3838)**.

Center for Faith and Opportunity Initiative (CFOI): The CFOI is an office located in the VA Office of Public and Intergovernmental Affairs. Their mission is to engage, educate and inform faith-based, community, and non-profit organizations about the VA tools and resources that will equip them to better serve the Veterans, their families, survivors, caregivers, and beneficiaries within their organizations. The VA Center for Faith participates in numerous outreach events to partner with organizations that serve our nation's Veterans. During their partnership events, they bring a broad spectrum of VA resources and information through breakout sessions that include Veteran E-Benefits, survivors assistance, Veteran homelessness, opioid epidemic, and suicide prevention training by a trained VA suicide prevention coordinator. We encourage you to help to reach the over 20 million Veterans by partnering with them to host an event, through volunteering, coordinating clergy specific suicide prevention training, or learning how to establish a Veterans welcome center/ministry. For additional information please visit https://www.va.gov/cfbnpartnerships/.

VA Benefits for Veterans Living Overseas: VA monetary benefits, including disability compensation, pension, educational benefits, and burial allowances, are generally payable overseas. Some programs are restricted. Home loan guaranties are available only in the United States and selected U.S. territories and possessions. The Specially Adapted Housing benefit is available outside of the continental United States. Educational benefits are limited to approved, degree granting programs in institutions of higher learning. Beneficiaries living in foreign countries should contact the nearest American embassy or consulate for help. In Canada, contact an office of Veterans Affairs. For information, visit: https://www.benefits.va.gov/PERSONA/veteran-abroad.asp.

Incarcerated Veterans: VA service-connected disability compensation benefits are affected if a Veteran is convicted of a **felony** and incarcerated for more than 60 days. VA non-service connected pension benefits are affected if a Veteran is convicted of a **felony** or **misdemeanor** and incarcerated for more than 60 days. Disability compensation paid to an incarcerated Veteran rated 20 percent or more disabled is limited to the 10 percent rate. For a Veteran whose disability rating is 10 percent, the payment is reduced to half of the rate payable to a Veteran evaluated as 10 percent disabled. Payments are not reduced for participants in work-release programs, residing in halfway houses, or under community control. Disability, death or survivor pension paid to a Veteran or beneficiary incarcerated following conviction of a felony or misdemeanor must be discontinued.

Benefits **not** paid to a Veteran or surviving spouse while incarcerated may be apportioned to eligible dependents. Failure to notify VA of a Veteran or beneficiary's incarceration can result in overpayment of benefits and the subsequent loss of all VA financial benefits until the overpayment is recovered.

Note: VA benefits will not be provided to any Veteran, survivor or dependent wanted for an outstanding felony warrant.

The Health Care for Re-Entry Veterans (HCRV) Program: The HCRV Program offers outreach, referrals, and short-term case management assistance for incarcerated Veterans who may be at risk for homelessness upon their release. To locate an outreach worker please visit: https://www.va.gov/homeless/reentry.asp.

The Veterans Justice Outreach Program (VJO): The VJO Program provides outreach and linkage to needed treatment and services to Veterans involved in law enforcement encounters, seen in the court system, and/or incarcerated in local jails who may be at risk for homelessness upon their release. To locate a Veterans Justice Outreach Specialist, please visit: http://www.va.gov/HOMELESS/VJO.asp.

Veterans of Operation Enduring Freedom, Iraqi Freedom, and New Dawn (OEF/OIF/OND): VA has personnel stationed at major military hospitals to help seriously injured service members returning from Operations Enduring Freedom, Iraqi Freedom, and New Dawn (OEF/OIF/ OND) as they transition from military to civilian life. OEF/ OIF/OND service members who have questions about VA benefits or need assistance filing a VA claim or accessing services can contact the nearest VA office or call **1-800-827-1000**.

VOW to Hire Heroes Act: The Act made Transition Assistance Program (TAP), including attendance at VA benefit briefings, mandatory for most service members transitioning to civilian status; upgraded career counseling options, focused TAP more heavily on job hunting skills, and tailored the program for the 21st century job market. The Act allows service members to begin the post-military employment process prior to separation or retirement from military service. This enhances opportunities to connect transitioning service members to both private-sector employers and Federal agencies seeking to hire Veterans. It also provides disabled Veterans up to one year of additional vocational rehabilitation and employment benefits. The Act provides tax credits for hiring Veterans and disabled Veterans who are out of work.

Transition Assistance Program (TAP): TAP consists of comprehensive workshops at military installations designed to assist service members as they transition from military to civilian life. A critical component of TAP is Transition GPS (Goals, Plans, Success); an outcome-based, modular curriculum with standardized learning objectives that transforms the way the military prepares service members separating from Active Duty to pursue their post-service career goals. It is designed to help service members depart military service "career ready" and meet mandatory Career Readiness Standards (CRS), regardless of their branch of service. VA collaborates with the Department of Defense to align TAP offerings with the current Military Life Cycle framework, which embeds transition planning and preparation for meeting career-readiness standards throughout a service member's military career.

The intent is for VA to utilize these touchpoints with service members throughout the Military Life Cycle to provide key information that service members need at each step to ensure they are ready for a successful transition. Retiring service members are allowed to attend Transition GPS up to 24 months prior to retirement, while separating service members can attend up to 12 months prior to separating. VA benefit briefings are comprised of two briefings focusing on benefits and services service members have earned through their service. Additionally, service members have the opportunity to participate in one or more two-day tailored tracks within Transition GPS curriculum to meet their personal career goals: Accessing Higher Education, for those pursuing a college education; Career Technical Training, for those seeking industry-recognized credentials in shorter-term training programs; or Entrepreneurship, for those wanting to start their own business. Service members can also sign up for one-on-one appointments with a VA representative; interested service members should contact their local TAP manager to sign up for this program.

In-Transition: In-Transition is a free, voluntary program with coaches who provide psychological health care support to service members, Veterans, and their health care providers during times of transition. This program provides access to transitional support, motivation, and healthy lifestyle assistance and advice from qualified coaches through the toll-free telephone number 1-800-424-7877. For more information, visit: http://intransition.dcoe.mil.

Federal Recovery Coordination Program (FRCP): The FRCP assists severely wounded, ill, or injured service members, Veterans, and their families. Federal Recovery Coordinators (FRCs) are located at both VA and Department of Defense (DoD) facilities, and provide virtual care coordination and advocacy services regardless of client location, medical treatment, geographic location of injury, place of medical diagnosis, or military or Veteran status. FRCs provide client centric services that assist with coordinating benefits, services, and care which are aligned with client goals for recovery, rehabilitation, and reintegration. The program is open to clients who may have one or more of the following problems: Traumatic Brain Injury; Post-Traumatic Stress Disorder; Spinal Cord Injury; Burns; Amputation; Blindness of Visual Impairments; an at risk for psychological complications If you think you may qualify, know someone who may qualify or desire additional information, please contact the FRCP at 877-732-4456.

Pre-Separation Counseling through Military Service: Service members may receive pre-separation counseling 24 months prior to retirement or 12 months prior to separation from active duty. These sessions present information on education, training, employment assistance, National Guard and Reserve programs, medical benefits, and financial assistance.

Verification of Military Experience and Training (VMET): The VMET Document, DD Form 2586, helps service members verify previous experience and training to potential employers, negotiate credits at schools, and obtain certificates or licenses. VMET documents are available only through each military branch's support office and are intended for service members who have at least six months of active duty. Service members should obtain VMET documents from their Transition Support Office within 12 months of separation or 24 months of retirement.

Veterans' Workforce Investment Program: Recently separated Veterans and those with service-connected disabilities, significant barriers to employment, or who served on active duty during a period in which a campaign or expedition badge was authorized, can contact the nearest state employment office for employment help through the Veterans Workforce Investment Program. The program may be conducted through state or local public agencies, community organizations or private, non-profit organizations.

Veteran Employment Services Office (VESO): VESO provides professional coaching, primarily to Veterans seeking employment in the Department of Veterans Affairs, by teaching Veterans how to maximize their military skills to match the Department's critical staffing needs. VESO helps Veterans in understanding the Federal hiring process through virtual training opportunities such as: Writing Your Federal Resume; Navigating Through USAjobs.gov; and Interview Techniques. VEO advocates and brings awareness of the Department's Veteran Employment Initiatives specifically designed for disabled Veterans to increase employment opportunities. They help to support Veteran employees retention in the Department's workforce by advocating for their career advancement in accordance with merit promotion principles and laws. For more information please visit www.vaforvets.va.gov and follow us on: www.facebook.com/Veso.VAforVets.

State Employment Services: Veterans can find employment information, education and training opportunities, job counseling, job search workshops, and resume preparation assistance by visiting their individual State Department of Veteran Affairs. Many states have Veterans Employment Centers, at state Workforce Career or One-Stop Centers. These offices also have specialists to help disabled Veterans find employment. Additional information and access to services are available at https://www.va.gov/careers-employment/.

Unemployment Compensation: Veterans who do not begin civilian employment immediately after leaving military service may receive weekly unemployment compensation for a limited time. The amount and duration of payments are determined by individual states. Apply by contacting the nearest state employment office listed in the local telephone directory.

Veterans Preference for Federal Jobs: Since the time of the Civil War, Veterans of the Armed Forces have been given some degree of preference in appointments to federal jobs. Veterans' preference in its present form comes from the Veterans' Preference Act of 1944, as amended, and now codified in Title 5, United States Code (U.S.C.). By law, Veterans who are disabled or who served on active duty during certain specified time periods or in military campaigns are entitled to preference over others when hiring from competitive lists of eligible candidates, and also in retention during a reduction in force.

To receive preference, a Veteran must have been discharged or released from active duty under honorable conditions or received a general discharge. Preference is also provided for certain widows and widowers of deceased Veterans who died in service, spouses of service-connected disabled Veterans, and mothers of Veterans who died under honorable conditions on active duty or have permanent and total service-connected disabilities.

Enrolled Veterans can print a copy of their preference letter from the eBenefits portal. For more information about Veterans Preference, please visit: www.usajobs.gov, https://www.va.gov/careers-employment/.

Veterans' Recruitment Appointment: Veterans' recruitment appointment allows federal agencies to appoint eligible Veterans to jobs without competition. These appointments can be converted to career or career conditional positions after two years of satisfactory work. Veterans should apply directly to the agency where they wish to work. For additional information on Veterans Recruitment Appointment, please visit: https://www.va.gov/careers-employment/.

Small Businesses: VA's Center for Verification and Evaluation (CVE) helps Veterans interested in forming or expanding small businesses, and helps VA contracting offices identify Veteran-owned small businesses. For additional information call toll-free at: 1-866-584-2344 or visit: https://www.va.gov/osdbu/.

Like other federal agencies, VA is required to place a portion of its contracts and purchases with small and disadvantaged businesses. VA has a special office to help small and disadvantaged businesses get information on VA acquisition opportunities. For additional information call toll-free at: 1-800-949-8387 or visit: https://www.va.gov/osdbu/ or write to the:

> U.S. Department of Veterans Affairs
> Office of Small Business (OOSB)
> 810 Vermont Avenue,
> N.W. Washington, DC 20420-0001

Dependents & Survivors Health Care - Civilian Health and Medical Program of the Department of Veterans Affairs (CHAMPVA): Under CHAMPVA, certain dependents and survivors can receive reimbursement for most medical expenses – inpatient, outpatient, mental health, prescription medication, skilled nursing care and durable medical equipment.

To be eligible for CHAMPVA, an individual cannot be eligible for TRICARE (the medical program for civilian dependents provided by DoD) and must be one of the following: the spouse or child of a Veteran whom VA has rated permanently and totally disabled due to a service-connected disability **or** the surviving spouse or child of a Veteran, who died from a VA-rated service-connected disability, or who, at the time of death, was rated permanently and totally disabled **or** the surviving spouse or child of a Veteran who died on active duty service and in the line of duty, not due to misconduct.

However, in most cases, these family members are eligible for TRICARE, not CHAMPVA. A surviving spouse under age 55 who remarries loses CHAMPVA eligibility at midnight of the date on remarriage. He/she may re-establish eligibility if the remarriage ends by death, divorce or annulment effective the first day of the month following the termination of the remarriage or December 1, 1999, whichever is later. A surviving spouse who remarries after age 55 does not lose eligibility upon remarriage.

For those who have Medicare entitlement or other health insurance, CHAMPVA is a secondary payer. Beneficiaries with Medicare must be enrolled in Parts A&B to maintain CHAMPVA eligibility. For additional information please call **1-800-733-8387** or visit: https://www.va.gov/COMMUNITYCARE/programs/dependents/champva/champva_eligibility.asp, or write:

Chief Business Office Purchased Care
VA Health Administration Center, CHAMPVA
P.O. Box 469028
Denver, CO 80246

Key Information for Family Members about the Affordable Care Act:
The Affordable Care Act, also known as the health care law, was created to expand access to affordable health care coverage to all Americans, lower costs, and improve quality and care coordination. Under the health care law, people will have health coverage that meets a minimum standard (called "minimum essential coverage") by Jan. 1, 2014 or qualify for an exemption, or pay a fee when filing their taxes, if they have affordable options but remain uninsured.

VA wants all Veterans and their families to receive health care that improves their health and well-being. Dependents and/survivors enrolled in the Civilian Health and Medical Program of the Department of Veterans Affairs (CHAMPVA) or the Spina Bifida Health Care Program meet the requirement to have health care coverage under the health care law and do not need to take any additional steps. The law does not change CHAMPVA or Spina Bifida benefits, access or costs. Veterans' family members who do not have coverage that meets the health care law's standard should consider their options through the Health Insurance Marketplace, which is a new way to shop for and purchase private health insurance. For more information about the Health Insurance Marketplace, visit http://www.healthcare.gov or call **1-800-318-2596**. For additional information about the VA and the health care law, visit http://www.va.gov/aca or call **1-877-222-VETS (8387)**.

Dependents & Survivors Benefits - Death Gratuity Payment: Military services provide payment, called a death gratuity, in the amount of $100,000 to the next of kin of service members who die while on active duty (including those who die within 120 days of separation) as a result of service-connected injury or illness. If there is no surviving spouse or child, then parents or siblings designated as next of kin by the service member may be provided the payment. The payment is made by the last military command of the deceased. If the beneficiary is not paid automatically, application may be made to the military service concerned.

Dependency and Indemnity Compensation (DIC): DIC is a tax-free monetary benefit generally payable to eligible survivors of military service members who died in the line of duty or eligible survivors of Veterans whose death resulted from a service-related injury or disease. DIC may also be paid to certain survivors of Veterans who were totally disabled from service –connected conditions at the time of death, even though their service connected disabilities did not cause their deaths. The survivor qualifies if the Veteran was:

1. Continuously rated totally disabled for a period of 10 years immediately preceding death; or

2. Continuously rated totally disabled from the date of military discharge and for at least 5 years immediately preceding death; or

3. A former POW who was continuously rated totally disabled for a period of at least one year immediately preceding death.

4. For more detailed information, visit http://www.benefits.va.gov/COMPENSATION/types-dependency_and_indemnity.asp.

DIC Eligibility (Surviving Spouse): To qualify for DIC, a surviving spouse must meet the following requirements:

- married to a service member who died on active duty, active duty for training, or inactive duty training, or

- validly married the Veteran before Jan. 1, 1957, or

- married the Veteran within 15 years of discharge from the period of military service in which the disease or injury that caused the Veteran's death began or was aggravated, or

- was married to the Veteran for a least one year, or

- had a child with the Veteran, and cohabitated with the Veteran continuously until the Veteran's death, or

- if separated, was not at fault for the separation, and is not currently remarried.

Note: A surviving spouse who remarried on or after Dec.16, 2003, and on or after attaining age 57, is entitled to continue to receive DIC.

DIC Eligibility (Surviving Child): Not included on the surviving spouse's DIC, AND Unmarried, AND Under age 18, or between the ages of 18 and 23 and attending school at an approved institution.

Note: A child adopted out of the Veteran's family may be eligible for DIC if all other eligibility criteria are met.

DIC Eligibility (Surviving Parent): VA provides an income-based monthly benefit to the surviving parent(s) of a service member or Veteran whose death was service-related. When countable income exceeds the limit set by law, no benefits are payable. The spouse's income must also be included if the parent is living with a spouse.

DIC and Aid and Attendance/Housebound Benefits: If a Veteran died on or after Jan. 1, 1993, his or her surviving spouse may receive additional benefits beyond the basic DIC rate if he or she is residing in a skilled nursing facility, require the regular assistance of another person to perform the activities of daily living, or if he or she is permanently housebound. This additional benefit is referred to as "Aid and Attendance" or "Housebound."

DIC 8-Year Special Allowance: If a deceased Veteran was considered "permanent and totally disabled"(either by 100 percent rating or permanent and total individual unemployability) for eight (8) continuous years prior to death, his/her surviving spouse may be entitled to an additional amount of $272.46 monthly on the DIC award effective Dec. 1, 2017. If there are any surviving dependent children under age 18 in the care of the surviving spouse, an additional $270.00 effective Dec. 1, 2017 may be further added to the DIC award for the initial two (2) years of entitlement. This additional amount will be automatically terminated two years after the DIC award grant.

Restored Entitlement Program for Survivors: An additional special benefit may be payable to Survivors of a Veteran who died of service-connected causes prior to Aug. 13, 1981. The amount of the benefit is based on information provided by the Social Security Administration.

Survivors Pension: Survivors Pension is a tax-free benefit payable to low-income surviving spouses or children who have not married/ remarried since the death of the Veteran. Survivors Pension is an income-based program, and any benefit payable is reduced by annual income from other sources, such as Social Security. If the Survivor has unreimbursed medical expenses, these costs can be deducted from countable income to increase the benefit amount (such as cost of care at an Assisted Living or Skilled Nursing Facility).

To be eligible for Survivor's Pension, the deceased Veteran must have met the following requirements:

1.   If the Veteran served on or before Sept. 7, 1980, he/she must have served at least 90 days of active military service, with at least one day during a war time period.

2.   If the Veteran entered active duty after Sept. 7, 1980, the Veteran generally must have served at least 24 months or the full tour of duty with at least one day during a war time period.

3.   Discharged from military service under other than dishonorable conditions.

To qualify as a surviving child of a deceased Veteran, the child must meet the following requirements: under age 18 or under age 23 if attending a VA-approved school or permanently incapable of self-support due to a disability diagnosed before age 18. Additional information on pension benefits is available at https://www.benefits.va.gov/pension/. To apply, complete VA Form 21P-534EZ and mail it to the Pension Management Center (PMC) of jurisdiction.

Note: Survivors pension provides a monthly payment to bring an eligible person's income to a level established by law. The payment is reduced by the annual income from other sources such as Social Security.

Survivors Aid and Attendance and Housebound Benefits: Survivors who are eligible for pension and require the aid and attendance of an-other person, or are housebound, may be eligible for a higher maximum pension rate. These additional benefits cannot be paid without eligibility to pension. An eligible individual may qualify if he or she requires the regular aid of another person in order to perform personal functions re-quired for everyday living, is bedridden, a patient in a nursing home due to mental or physical incapacity, blind, or permanently and substantially confined to his/her immediate premises because of a disability.

To apply for aid and attendance or housebound benefits, submit a VA Form 21-2680, Examination for Housebound Status or Permanent

Need for Regular Aid and Attendance to the nearest Regional Office or PMC.

Please include copies of any evidence, preferably a report from an attending physician or a nursing home, validating the need for aid and attendance or housebound status. The report should contain sufficient detail to determine whether there is disease or injury producing physical or mental impairment, loss of coordination, or conditions affecting the ability to dress and undress, to feed oneself, to attend to sanitary needs, and to keep oneself ordinarily clean and presentable, or whether confined to the immediate premises due to disability.

Children of Women Vietnam Veterans Born with Certain Birth Defects: Biological children of women Veterans who served in Vietnam at any time during the period beginning on Feb. 28, 1961, and ending on May 7, 1975, may be eligible for certain benefits because of birth defects associated with the mother's service in Vietnam that resulted in a permanent physical or mental disability.

The covered birth defects do not include conditions due to family disorders, birth-related injuries, or fetal or neonatal infirmities with well-established causes. A monetary allowance is paid at one of four disability levels based on the child's degree of permanent disability.

Appeals of VA Claims Decisions: Veterans and other claimants for VA benefits have the right to appeal decisions made by VA. The most common issues appealed are disability compensation, pension, education benefits, recovery of overpayments, reimbursement for unauthorized medical services, and denial of burial and memorial benefits. A claimant has one year from the date of the notification of a VA decision to file an appeal. The first step in the appeal process is for a claimant to file a written notice of disagreement with the VA department that made the decision. Following receipt of the written notice, VA will furnish the claimant a "Statement of the Case" describing what facts, laws, and regulations were used in deciding the case. To complete the request for appeal, the claimant must file a "Substantive Appeal" within 60 days of the mailing of the Statement of the Case, or within one year from the date VA mailed its decision, whichever period ends later.

Board of Veterans' Appeals: The Board is a component of VA this is the Secretary's designee to decide appeals from all three Administrations, also called AOJs – VBA, VHA, and NCA. The Board's mission is to conduct hearings with appellants and decide appeals properly before it in a timely manner. The Board's jurisdiction extends to all questions in a matter involving a decision by the Secretary under the law that affects a provision of benefits and services by the Secretary to Veterans, their dependents, or their survivors.

U.S. Court of Appeals for Veterans Claims: A final Board decision that does not grant a claimant the benefits desired may be appealed to the U.S. Court of Appeals for Veterans Claims. The court is an independent body, not part of the Department of Veterans Affairs.

Notice of an appeal must be received by the court with a postmark that is within 120 days after the Board mailed its decision. The court reviews the record considered by the Board. It does not hold trials or receive new evidence. Appellants may represent themselves before the court or have lawyers or approved agents as representatives. Oral argument is held only at the direction of the court. Either party may appeal a decision of the court to the U.S. Court of Appeals for the Federal Circuit and may seek review in the Supreme Court of the United States. Published decisions, case status information, rules and procedures, and other special announcements can be found at http://www.uscourts.cavc.gov/. The court's decisions can also be found in West's Veterans Appeals Reporter, and on the Westlaw and LEXIS online services. For questions, call (202) 501-5970 or write to:

Clerk of the Court
625 Indiana Ave. NW, Suite 900
Washington, DC 20004

Replacement of Military Medals and Records: Medals awarded while in active service are issued by the individual military services if requested by Veterans or their next of kin. Requests for replacement medals, decorations, and awards should be directed to the branch of the military in which the Veteran served. However, for Air Force (including Army Air Corps) and Army Veterans, the National Personnel Records Center (NPRC) verifies awards and forwards requests and verification to appropriate services. Requests for replacement medals should be submitted on Standard Form 180, "Request Pertaining to Military Records," which may be obtained at VA offices or the Internet at www.va.gov/vaforms/. Forms, addresses, and other information on requesting medals can be found on the Military Personnel Records section of NPRC's Website at http://www. archives.gov/stlouis/militarypersonnel/index.html. For questions, call

Military Personnel Records at **(314) 801-0800**, or email questions to: MPR.center@nara.gov.

When requesting medals, type or clearly print the Veteran's full name, include the Veteran's branch of service, service number or Social Security number, and provide the Veteran's exact or approximate dates of military service. The request must contain the signature of the Veteran or next of kin if the Veteran is deceased. If available, include a copy of the discharge or separation document, WDAGO Form 53-55 or DD Form 214. If discharge or separation documents are lost, Veterans or the next of kin of deceased Veterans may obtain duplicate copies through the eBenefits portal (www.ebenefits.va.gov) or by completing forms found on the Internet at http://www.archives.gov/research/index.html and mailing or faxing them to the NPRC, or alternatively, write to:

National Personnel Records Center, Military Personnel Records
1 Archives Drive
St. Louis, MO 63138-1002.

Specify that a duplicate separation document is needed. The Veteran's full name should be printed or typed so that it can be read clearly, but the request must also contain the signature of the Veteran or the signature of the next of kin, if the Veteran is deceased. Include the Veteran's branch of service, service number or Social Security number, and exact or approximate dates and years of service. Use Standard Form 180, "Request Pertaining to Military Records." It is not necessary to request a duplicate copy of a Veteran's discharge or separation papers solely for the purpose of filing a claim for VA benefits. If complete information about the Veteran's service is furnished on the application, VA will obtain verification of service.

Correcting Military Records: The Secretary of a military department, acting through a Board for Correction of Military Records, has authority to change any military record when necessary to correct an error or remove an injustice. A correction board may consider applications for correction of a military record, including a review of a discharge issued by court-martial. Application is made with DD Form 149, available at VA offices, Veterans organizations or visit http://www.dtic.mil/whs/directives/forms/ dd/ddforms0001-0499.htm.

Review of Discharge from Military Service: Each of the military services maintains a discharge review board with authority to change correct or modify discharges or dismissals not issued by a sentence of a general court-martial. The board has no authority to address medical discharges. If the Veteran is deceased or incompetent, the surviving spouse, next of kin or legal representative, may apply for a review of discharge by writing to the military department concerned, using DD Form 293, "Application for the Review of Discharge from the Armed Forces of the United States." This form may be obtained at a VA regional office, from Veterans organizations or online at http://www.dtic.mil/whs/directives/forms/dd/ddforms0001-0499.htm.

However, if the discharge was more than 15 years ago, a Veteran must petition the appropriate Service's Board for Correction of Military Records using DD Form 149, "Application for Correction of Military Records Under the Provisions of Title 10, U.S. Code, Section 1552." A discharge review is conducted by a review of an applicant's record and, if requested, by a hearing before the board.

Discharges awarded as a result of a continuous period of unauthorized absence in excess of 180 days make persons ineligible for VA benefits regardless of action taken by discharge review boards, unless VA determines there were compelling circumstances for the absence. Boards for the Correction of Military Records also may consider such cases. Veterans with disabilities incurred or aggravated during active duty may qualify for medical or related benefits regardless of separation and characterization of service. Veterans separated administratively under other than honorable conditions may request that their discharge be reviewed for possible re-characterization, provided they file their appeal within 15 years of the date of separation. Questions regarding the review of a discharge should be addressed to the appropriate discharge review board at the address listed on DD Form 293.

Physical Disability Board of Review: Veterans separated due to disability from Sept. 11, 2001, through Dec. 31, 2009, with a combined rating of 20 percent or less, as determined by the respective branch of service Physical Evaluation Board (PEB), and not found eligible for retirement, may be eligible for a review by the Physical Disability Board of Review (PDBR).

The PDBR was established to reassess the accuracy and fairness of certain PEB decisions, and where appropriate, recommend the correction of discrepancies and errors. A PDBR review will not lower the disability rating previously assigned by the PEB, and any correction may be made retroactively to the day of the original disability separation. As a result of the request for review by the PDBR, no further relief from the Board of Corrections of Military Records may be sought, and the recommendation by the PDBR, once accepted by the respective branch of service, is final. A comparison of these two boards, along with other PDBR information, can be viewed at http://www.health.mil/pdbr.

Low Income Home Energy Assistance Program (LIHEAP): The U.S. Department of Health and Human Services provides funding to states to help low-income households with their heating and home energy costs under the Low Income Home Energy Assistance Program (LIHEAP). LIHEAP can also assist with insulating homes to make them more energy efficient and reduce energy costs. The LIHEAP program in your community determines if your household's income qualifies for the program. To find out where to apply, call **1-866-674-6327** or e-mail energy@ncat.org 7 a.m. - 5 p.m. (Mountain Time). More information can be found at https://www.acf.hhs.gov/ocs/programs/liheap.

Burial and Memorial Benefits

VA operates 136 national cemeteries, of which 78 are currently open for both new casket and cremation interments, and 17 may accept new interments of cremated remains only. Burial options are limited to those available at a specific cemetery and may include in-ground casket, or interment of cremated remains in a columbarium, in ground, or in a scattering area. For more information, visit the National Cemetery Administration website at http://www.cem.va.gov.

Burial in VA National Cemeteries

Burial in a national cemetery is open to all members of the Armed Forces, and Veterans who have met minimum active duty service requirements, and were discharged under conditions other than dishonorable.

Members of the Reserve components of the Armed Forces who die while on active duty, while on training duty or were eligible for retired pay, or were called to active duty and served the full term of service for which they were called, may also be eligible for burial.

Their surviving spouse, minor children, and, under certain conditions, unmarried adult children with disabilities, may also be eligible for burial. Eligible spouses and children may be buried even if they predecease the Veteran.

With certain exceptions, eligibility for burial based on active duty service be-ginning after Sept. 7, 1980, as an enlisted person, and after Oct.16, 1981, as an officer, must have been for a minimum of 24 consecutive months or the full period of active duty (as in the case of reservists or National Guard members called to active duty for a limited duration). Active duty for training, by itself, while serving in the Reserves or National Guard, is not sufficient to confer eligibility. Reservists and National Guard members, as well as their spouses and dependent children, are eligible if they were entitled to retired pay at the time of death, or would have been upon reaching the requisite age.

VA may bar eligible individuals from receiving burial and memorial benefits if they are found to have committed serious federal or state crimes or serious sex offenses. Such benefits include burial in a VA national cemetery, and receipt of a government-furnished headstone, marker, medallion, burial flag, and Presidential Memorial Certificate. Veterans and other claimants for VA burial benefits have the right to appeal decisions made by VA regarding eligibility for burial and memorial benefits. Readers with questions on the appeals process may contact the nearest VA national cemetery listed at http://www.cem.va.gov/cem/cems/listcem.asp or by calling 800-827-1000.

Surviving spouses of Veterans who died on or after Jan. 1, 2000 do not lose eligibility for burial in a national cemetery if they remarry.

Unmarried dependent children of Veterans who are under 21 years of age, or under 23 years of age if a full-time student at an approved edu-cational institution, are eligible for burial. Unmarried adult children who become physically or mentally disabled and incapable of self-support before age 21, or age 23 if a full-time student, may also be eligible.

Certain parents of Veterans who die due to hostile activity or from combat training-related injuries may be eligible for burial in a national cemetery with their child. The biological or adopted parents of a service member who died in combat or while performing training in preparation for a combat mission, who leaves no surviving spouse or dependent child, may be buried with the deceased service member if there is avail-able space. Eligibility is limited to those who died on or after Oct. 7, 2001, and biological or adoptive parents who died on or after Oct. 13, 2010.

The next of kin or authorized representative (e.g., funeral director) may make interment arrangements at the time of need by contact-ing the National Cemetery Scheduling Office at (800) 535-1117 or NCA.Scheduling@va.gov or, in some cases, the national cemetery in which burial is desired. VA does not normally conduct burials on weekends. Gravesites cannot be reserved; however, VA will honor reservations made before 1973 by the Department of the Army.

Pre-Need Burial Eligibility Determination: VA implemented the Preneed Burial Eligibility Determination Program to assist individuals interested in determining their eligibility for burial in a VA national cemetery.

Through this program, Veterans and their eligible family members can plan to use VA burial benefits that Veterans have earned through their military service. Planning in advance for a Veteran's or loved-one's final resting place can eliminate unnecessary delays during a family's time of bereavement. Veteran families will have increased confidence that their loved ones are eligible for burial in a VA national cemetery at their time of need.

To apply, individuals must submit VA Form 40-10007, Application for Pre-Need Determination of Eligibility for Burial in a VA National Cemetery (available at http://www.va.gov/vaforms/), to the National Cemetery Scheduling Office by faxing to 1-855-840-8299, or by mailing to the National Cemetery Scheduling Office, P.O. Box 510543, St. Louis, MO 63151. For more details, visit https://www.cem.va.gov/cem/pre-need/index.asp.

Burial Headstones and Markers: VA is authorized to furnish, upon request, an inscribed headstone or marker for the unmarked grave of an eligible decedent at any national, state Veterans, tribal, or private cemetery. VA will deliver a headstone or marker at no cost, anywhere in the world. For Medal of Honor (MOH) recipients, VA is authorized to provide a supplemental headstone or marker if the recipient served in the Armed Forces on or after April 6, 1917, and is eligible for a headstone or marker (or would be but for the individual's date of death), even if the grave is already marked with a private headstone or marker. For eligible Veterans (who are not MOH recipients) buried in a private cemetery whose deaths occurred on or after Nov. 1, 1990, VA may furnish a government headstone or marker even if the grave is already marked with a private one.

Spouses and dependent children are eligible for a government headstone or marker only if they are buried in a national or state Veterans cemetery.

Before requesting a headstone or marker for use in a private cemetery, eligible applicants should check with the cemetery to ensure the government-furnished headstone or marker will be accepted.

Those who may apply for burial headstones and markers include the decedent's spouse or individual in a legal union with the decedent; the decedent's child; parent or sibling; whether biological; adopted or step relation; and any lineal or collateral descendant of the decedent; personal representative Veterans Service Organization, individual employed by state or local government responsible for serving Veteran; individuals with legal responsibility for the disposition of the unclaimed remains of the decedent or other matters related to interment or memorialization, or anyone if the decedent's dates of service ended prior to April 6, 1917 (applies to others whose eligibility is derived). All installation fees at private cemeteries are the responsibility of the applicant.

Memorial Markers: VA provides memorial headstones and markers for placement in a national cemetery, a Veterans cemetery owned by a state or in the case of a Veteran, in a state, tribal, local or private cemetery with "IN MEMORY OF" as the first line of inscription for those whose remains are unavailable for burial. Remains that are unavailable for burial are those that have not been recovered or identified, were buried at sea, donated to science or cremated and scattered completely. Only eligible Veterans are authorized to receive memorial headstones or markers for use in private cemeteries; memorial headstones and markers are not authorized for placement in tribal cemeteries (including Veterans). For memorial headstone or marker requests, applicants must be a member of the decedent's family (spouse, individual in a legal union with the decedent, child, parent, or sibling, whether biological, adopted, or step-relation, and any lineal or collateral descendant of the decedent).

To submit a claim for a headstone or marker, or for a memorial marker for placement in a private cemetery, use VA Form 40-1330, Claim for Standard Government Headstone or Marker (available at http://www.va.gov/vaforms/) and provide a copy of the Veteran's military discharge documents or proof of military service. Claims sent without supporting documents will be delayed until eligibility can be determined. Mail the completed form and supporting documents to Memorial Products Service, Department of Veterans Affairs, 5109 Russell Road, Quantico, VA 22134-3903. The form and supporting documents may also be faxed toll free to 1-800-455-7143.

Inscriptions: Headstones and markers must be inscribed with the name of the deceased, branch of service, and year of birth and death. They also may be inscribed with other optional information, including an emblem of belief and, space permitting, additional text including military rank; war service such as "WORLD WAR II"; complete date of birth and death; military awards; military organizations; civilian or Veteran affiliations; and personalized words of endearment.

Medallion in lieu of government headstone or marker for private cemeteries: For decedents who served in the U.S. Armed Forces on or after April 6, 1917, and are eligible for VA memorialization benefits (or would be but for date of death), VA is authorized to provide a medallion instead of a headstone or marker if the grave is in a private cemetery and already marked with a privately-purchased headstone or marker. The VA medallion denotes the decedents' status as a Veteran. The Medal of Honor (MOH) Medallion is inscribed with "MEDAL OF HONOR" at the top and the branch of service at the bottom.

To submit a claim for a medallion to be affixed to a private headstone or marker in a private cemetery, use VA Form 40-1330M, Claim for Government Medallion for Placement in A Private Cemetery (available at http://www.va.gov/vaforms) and provide a copy of the Veteran's military discharge documents or proof of military service. Claims sent without supporting documents will be delayed until eligibility can be determined.

Mail the completed form and supporting documents to Memorial Products Service, Department of Veterans Affairs, 5109 Russell Road, Quantico, VA 22134-3903. The form and supporting documents may also be faxed toll free to 1-800-455-7143.

To check the status of a claim for a headstone or marker for placement in a national, state, or tribal Veterans cemetery, please call 202-565-4964. To check the status of one being placed in a private cemetery, please contact the Applicant Assistance Unit at 1-800-697-6947.

Other Memorialization

Presidential Memorial Certificates (PMCs): PMCs are issued to honor the memory of deceased persons whom VA finds eligible for burial in a national cemetery. This includes persons who died on active military, naval, or air service, members of Reserve components of the Armed Forces, including Army or Air National Guard, members of the Army, Navy, or Air Force Reserve Officers' Training Corps, or persons who at death were entitled to retired pay or would have been but for age.

Eligible recipients, including the next of kin, a relative, friend, or authorized service representative may request a PMC by mailing to Memorial Products Service (41B), Department of Veterans Affairs, 5109 Russell Road, Quantico, VA, 22134-3903, or faxing to 1-800-455-7143, a completed and signed VA Form 40-0247, Presidential Memorial Certificate Request Form, along with a copy of the Veteran's military discharge documents or proof of military service.

Requests sent without supporting documents will be delayed until eligibility can be determined. More information can be found at http://www.cem.va.gov/cem/pmc.asp.

Burial Flags: VA will furnish a U.S. burial flag to recognize deceased Veterans who received an other than dishonorable discharge. This includes certain persons who served in the organized military forces of the Commonwealth of the Philippines while in service of the U.S armed forces and who died on or after April 25, 1951. Also, eligible for a burial flag are Veterans who were entitled to retired pay for service in the Reserves or National Guard; or would have been entitled if over age 60; and members or former members of the Selected Reserve who served their initial obligation; or were discharged for a disability incurred or aggravated in the line of duty; or died while a member of the Selected Reserve. The next of kin may apply for the burial flag at any VA Regional Office or U.S. Post Office by completing VA Form 21-2008; Application for United States Flag for Burial Purposes. In most cases, a funeral director will help the family obtain the flag. For more information, visit http://www.cem.va.gov/cem/ burial_benefits/ burial_flags.asp.

Reimbursement of Burial Expenses: VA will pay a burial allowance up to $2,000 if the Veteran's death is service-connected. In such cases, the person who bore the Veteran's burial expenses may claim reimbursement from VA. In some cases, VA will pay the cost of transporting the remains of a Veteran whose death was service-connected to the nearest national cemetery with available gravesites. There is no time limit for filing reimbursement claims in service-connected death cases.

Burial Allowance: VA will pay a burial and funeral allowance of up to $2,000 for Veterans who die from service-connected injuries. VA will pay a burial and funeral allowance of up to $300 for Veterans who, at the time of death from nonservice-connected injuries, were entitled to receive pension or compensation or would have been entitled if they were not receiving military retirement pay. VA will pay a burial and funeral allowance of up to $762 when the Veteran's death occurs in a VA facility, a VA-contracted nursing home or a state Veterans nursing home. In cases in which the Veteran's death was not service-connected, claims must be filed within two years after burial or cremation.

Plot Allowance: VA will pay a plot allowance of up to $762 when a Veteran is buried in a cemetery not under U.S. government jurisdiction if:

- The Veteran was discharged from active duty because of disability incurred or aggravated in the line of duty;

- the Veteran was receiving compensation or pension or would have been if the Veteran was not receiving military retirement pay;

- or the Veteran died in a VA facility.

The plot allowance may be paid to the state for the cost of a plot or interment in a state-owned cemetery reserved solely for Veteran burials if the Veteran is buried without charge. Burial expenses paid by the deceased's employer or a state agency will not be reimbursed. For more information about burial and memorial benefits, please call 202-632-8035 or visit www.cem.va.gov/.

Veterans Cemeteries Administered by Other Agencies: The Department of the Army administers Arlington National Cemetery and other Army installation cemeteries. Eligibility is generally more restrictive than at VA national cemeteries. For information, call 703-607-8000; write Superintendent, Arlington National Cemetery, Arlington, VA 22211; or visit http://www.arlingtoncemetery.mil/about. The Department of the Interior's National Park Service maintains 14 national cemeteries located within larger park units. To view a list that includes overviews of these cemeteries, visit http://www.cem.va.gov/cems/doi.asp. Andersonville National Cemetery in Andersonville, Georgia, is the only one of these 14 cemeteries that is open to new interments within the national park boundaries. For more information, call 202-208-4747, or write Department of the Interior National Park Service, 1849 C Street, NW, Washington, DC 20240.

State and Tribal Veterans Cemeteries: There are currently 112 VA grant-funded Veterans cemeteries operating in 48 states, tribal organizations, and U.S. Territories that offer burial options for Veterans and their families. VA grant-funded cemeteries have similar eligibility requirements and certain states and tribal organizations may require state residency or tribal membership. Some services, particularly for family members, may require a fee. Contact the state or tribal Veterans cemetery or the state Veterans Affairs office for information. To locate a state or tribal Veterans cemetery, visit http://www.cem.va.gov/cem/grants/index.asp.

Unclaimed Veterans Remains: "Unclaimed Veterans" are defined as those who die with no next of kin to claim their remains and insufficient funds to cover burial expenses. In addition to burial in a VA national, VA-funded state or tribal Veterans cemetery and a government headstone or marker, there are monetary benefits associated with burial of unclaimed Veterans remains. These monetary benefits include reimbursement for the cost of the casket or urn used for burial, reimbursement for transportation to a national, state or tribal Veterans cemetery, and a burial allowance and plot allowance.

More information on memorial and monetary burial benefits for unclaimed Veterans remains can be found at http://www.cem.va.gov/cem/docs/factsheets/CasketUrnReimbursement.pdf. Applicants must submit VA Form 40-10088, Request for Reimbursement of Casket/Urn. For Veterans who die while at a VA facility under authorized VA admission or at a non-VA facility under authorized VA admission, and are unclaimed, the closest VA healthcare facility is responsible for arranging proper burial for the unclaimed Veteran.